ISBN: 978129038144

Published by:
HardPress Publishing
8345 NW 66TH ST #2561
MIAMI FL 33166-2626

Email: info@hardpress.net
Web: http://www.hardpress.net

TUMBLEFOLD

BY

JOSEPH
WHITTAKER

WITH A FOREWORD BY

BEN TILLETT, M.P.

NEW YORK

E. P. DUTTON & COMPANY

681 FIFTH AVENUE

PUBLISHED 1919,

By E. P. DUTTON & COMPANY

Printed in the United States of America

TO

WILLIAM JOHN BARWICK

The moonless nights of Tumblefold
Were lightened many a year ago
By dreams that I should some day know
The streets of London, paved with gold.

The dreams came true; to give or lend,
I hold a store of wealth divine,
Gleaned not from pavement, mart, nor mine,
But from such hearts as yours, Old Friend.

FOREWORD

By Ben Tillett, M.P.

THIS book is the sweetest human document I have ever heard of, or read. It is just a tale of Life's tragedies heroically borne—of a camaraderie almost romantic. It would be really romantic, but for the tragedy and meanness of it all. It is a glorification of what the superior person would call the "gutter snipe"—a gutter snipe pulsating with thoughts and feelings beyond his ken.

I know the neighbourhood in which the narrative is wrought. The author brings into vivid light what the actualities of the gutter life mean. We want books like these, and portrayals of slumland, that will not only shame us to sympathy, but will nerve us to resent the conditions imposed upon the helpless childhood of our country. It is sad, even too sad, to think that such conditions still exist.

The heroic fortitude of little Stubbs, Christ-like in its patience and beauty, is a figure standing aloof even from the mud and misery of Tumblefold; and the struggle of Motherhood, its fortitude, its relentless patience, compel an awesome respect—the unwept, unheard-of heroines of Motherhood, who have carried their cross—not for months, but for years—stand out a beautiful example to all that is superficially mean and selfish.

This book teems with character and beauty. If there be divinity in suffering the gall and wormwood and crown of thorns, then the romance of the Crucifixion makes all Life's history more pregnant with meaning than all the philosophy ever written.

A set of the proofs of "Tumblefold" were sent to me by an old comrade of many years' standing with the assurance that it had brought tears to his eyes. He asked me to write a Foreword to give a helping hand to the author, who I understand is a journalist on a suburban paper.

I have participated in many incidents similar to those described, and what strikes me as most remarkable is that nowhere throughout the book is there the least tinge of bitterness.

Considering his early life and struggles, Mr. Whittaker would have been justified had he dipped his pen in gall; but he has written a far more convincing book by virtue of his kindliness and restraint.

I can only thank him for a re-awakened memory of my own youth, hallowed and softened by time, for the refinement and kindliness he has imparted to his story, and above all for his intense humanity. His readers will be all the gladder, not merely to enjoy this book, but to understand how great a human document it is.

BEN TILLETT.

CONTENTS

TUMBLEFOLD

TUMBLEFOLD

CHAPTER I

INTRODUCTION

THIS is a book of memories; a plain, un-adorned story of a great friendship which was formed years ago among five schoolboys, of whom I was one.

That friendship and its memories are to me of the best that life has given me. It made a dark boyhood bearable and often happy for each one of us, and lit with hopeful possibilities what otherwise would have been inevitably a dubious and uncertain future. It is nothing ambitious, mind you, this book. Just the story of some of the infinite experiences in and out of school of five street urchins.

Street urchins? Yes. None of your public school boys, born of respectable parents, who roll up in carriages when school term begins, doing incredible deeds on the way with pop-guns and peashooters; whose school life is a long gorge of cake and lollypops, with occasional variations each day in the shape of lessons, interspersed with jokes at the expense of the French master. To say nothing of pillow-fights by night in the dormitories, and real fights by day with the town boys. No, your respectable public school boy has long ago had full justice done to him.

So by way of a change you have here the schoolboy experiences of five town boys.

The story should not be uninteresting on that account, though his words be weak and insufficient who tells it. For there is this: to each who wills to see it the halo of romance hangs in unsetting beauty over all child-life; as in the garden-encircled suburban villas, so in the squalidest streets and slums. And on these latter the glory is warmer, though subdued; contrasting as it does so weirdly with the darkness on which it falls.

We were reared in poverty. Only one who has lived in it knows the full significance of the word. He knows also how much strength of the truest and pathos of the saddest may be found in the lives of the poor.

You whose glib lips never tire of condemning the thriftless and improvident poor, ask yourselves this one question—Would you, in the same place and under the same conditions do, or be, any better? Would you be even as good?

Imagine yourself, any one Pharisee among you, as a labourer or an unskilled mechanic, earning twenty shillings for six days' work; and, for eight or nine months in the year, working only four or even three days a week: a female—your wife—and two or three children at home—yourself and her uneducated, yet possessing a world of undeveloped faculties—living in a dirty house in a foul court that the sun is ashamed to shine on—indulging in habits you know to be low and vile—starving half your time on bread and lard for breakfast, dinner, and supper, with an occasional dinner luxury, when in season, of beans and bacon—getting, it is true, when you are on full-time, a piece of meat for your Sunday dinner, a remnant usually bought on the verge of Saturday midnight from a cag-mag stall in the market.

Picture yourself with one patched cotton shirt to your back, and the relics of a suit of clothes to wear week-days and Sundays, and the female, your wife, even worse off than that —to say not a word of the childwrecks crawling on the floor. Stand you in that place for one moment, and look forward, with the other man's eyes, to a long stretch of weeks of semi-starvation, or unreasoning gorges during a few weeks of full-time; and, all along, the quarrels and the blows with the female, your wife, and the demoniac children; and always

the Saturday nights of beerswilling into oblivion. Think of all this, continued and continued till you feel yourself growing old, old
and hideous and weak; till the lights go out on
your path, starvation closes in on you and her,
and you move sullenly towards the hopeless
workhouse waiting, always waiting, at the end.
When, with your sons in jail and your daugh-
ters on the streets, you have nowhere else to
lay your heads, *that* is still left. So you go
there or die. It is much the same thing.

Seeing and knowing all this, you then might
change your mind.

.   .   .   .   .

We five were reared in poverty. Four of us
were born in it. We knew it, and we felt its
hurt; but for us there was no stigma, no disgrace, in being poor. We took it as a matter
of course, and in our way were not unhappy.
For the dearest prerogative of childhood is its
infinite faith in itself and life. Everything
seems fashioned to give it pleasure, and it looks
forward with a confident, wide-eyed vision
which can see in all the days to come no change
from so divine an order of things.

So, being boys, we lived, and enjoyed the
process, on plain, meagre fare, in thin, shabby
garments; we grew in a manner healthy and

hearty, had our games and our quarrels, our talks and our fights, and made merry in school-days or holidays, as is the fashion of all boys.

And hereafter comes the story of it, in no regular sequence of narrative, in no fixed order of dates. I am no writer, and could not give you an artistically constructed story even if I tried; and I do not mean to try.

For me, the bare past is enough, and I shall be satisfied if in these fragmentary memories of a past time I can give a plain, true outline of a not wholly uneventful history,

CHAPTER II

WE were five: Potter, Yeubrey, Stubbs, Ryder, and Jones. We were four at first. That was before Stubbs came.

We lived almost next door to each other in Tumblefold; a mysterious collection of dark alleys and passages, leading mostly nowhere. It is situated in the oldest portion of Wolverhampton, an ancient borough built on a range of low hills bordering the Black Country.

Our houses were part of a straggling block of six, at the street end of the Fold, considered to be the Respectable end. For Respectability was hankered after even in Tumblefold. The children in these houses each wore a best suit on Sundays, or at any rate a portion of one, with the mysterious assurance that the remainder lay in the box upstairs. If by any mischance the box could not be opened the children were ill, and stayed indoors all day.

6

Ah, that box upstairs! We found out soon enough where and up whose stairs it lay.

Heavy old buildings they were. Great beams ran across each ceiling, and their weight had long ago forced the walls out of the perpendicular into the queerest shapes. Yet they were warm, though old. You could sit round the fire, when you had one, and talk your loudest, with no uneasy fear of your next door neighbour hearing all you were saying, and learning your family secrets.

They had memories, too, these old houses in Tumblefold. They were at least three hundred years old, and when they were built Wolverhampton knew neither coalpits nor ironworks. They lay in the heart of a small country town, at the foot of a hill. On the hilltop still stands a fine old church whose age runs into four figures. When they were built they were pleasant, large houses at the foot of the old monks' gardens, and you had but to go to their diamond paned windows to see north, south, east, or west a wide stretch of green fields and meadows, smiling under a smokeless sky.

Now it is different. They are in the centre of a dirty old town. Ironworks, coalpits, and factories encircle them. All day long the smoke, and the endless din of traffic and machinery; all night the same stifling, chemically poisoned air. And poverty right through the town, and bitter indeed in Tumblefold.

. . . . .

We were four, as I said, at first, and were born and reared in Tumblefold. At five we could have threaded its winding passages blindfold. At the time our fellowship of five began our ages ranged from seven to eight.

Potter was a talkative lad, the son of a mechanic. His father was a first-class worker, but a heavy drinker, and poverty prevailed in their house.

The Ryders lived next door. They were a large family. The father worked in a warehouse for low wages. Ryder was a queer, angular-featured lad, the funny boy of our group; and was only prevented by a certain natural gravity, due to environment, from aspiring to be a clown.

Jones lived in a corner house. He was biggest of us, but not the oldest. A healthy, light-haired lad; good-humoured, but somehow always fighting.

The Yeubreys, of whom I was the youngest, lived in the other corner house, jutting on the main passage through the Fold. It was dignified by a gas-lamp, the only one, casting a dim but not religious light on the entrance to the labyrinth. A long gas pipe ran up the wall to it. On winter nights we four used to stand talking under our window, till, for want of something else to do, one of us would give the pipe a gentle kick. This invariably put out the light.

In a very few moments an unwary passer-by would tumble over the big block of basalt which formed the cornerstone of our house. His remarks would open several doors, and a volley of abuse would be poured on four invisible boys; what time the abusers were trying to relight the lamp by means of lighted paper tied to the end of a long stick, and four little boys were chuckling hilariously round a corner.

One morning we four, as usual, sallied through the Fold to school. We noticed with surprise that a house in a row just below ours was empty. We talked it over as we went along and returned the usual verdict: "A moonlight flit."

A day or two later, returning from afternoon school, we found the house occupied and a lorry-load of furniture at the door. After tea we stood outside looking on and criticising the furniture, which rather surprised us; and when we saw two cane-seated chairs taken in we decided that if there were any boys in the family we would at any rate see what they were like.

While we were talking one came out of the house, a thin little lad of about eight, wearing an overcoat, buttoned up, which was a bad sign. His face was pale, and girlish about the mouth. He wore a collar, however, which turned an unfavourable impression in his favour. We wore common scarves on week-days and collars on Sundays.

He came hesitatingly towards us. Jones stepped impressively up to him and said loudly, "Hello, you fresh kid, what's yer name?"

The stranger shrank back, and I noticed his eyes dilate with that expression of fear one sees in the eyes of animals under the knife.

A band of the "rough lot," as we called the other lads, saw it also, and grinned maliciously. One of them, a big lad with a dirty face, called Claydabber Dick because his father was a bricklayer's labourer, shouted out, "He's chicken-hearted. Give him one on his smeller, Jones."

In reply Jones turned round with, "Go an' wash yer dirty face, then come back an' I'll smash yer jimmy for yer."

Dick turned red, but did not show fight.

Jones looked at him, then opened his lips. We closed round. Slowly and calmly came the words which always forced a fight—

"Claydabber Dick,
Three farthin's a wik."

Two minutes later the fight was over and Claydabber was alternately weeping and holding the back of his hand to his nose to see if it still bled.   The innocent cause of the fight had disappeared.

Next morning, when we were in school, came a knock at the door.   The schoolmaster answered it and in a few minutes came back —with the stranger.   We waited anxiously and were somehow glad to see the master bring him to our class.   By sundry signs we got him in the middle of our desk and made free.   His name was Stubbs.   His father was dead.   They were once well-to-do, but were not so now; and his mother and two sisters supported themselves by washing and needlework.

He was a weak lad, was Freddy Stubbs, but as affectionate as a kitten.   And we, being fairly healthy, considering all things, took him among us and became his staunch protectors.

And so we were five.

CHAPTER III

CHILD-LIFE IN TUMBLEFOLD

TO child-life, Tumblefold was no Garden of Eden. It was dirty, it was dark, and the drains were nearly always choked; therefore it was seldom free from fevers. Its inhabitants, having few other pleasures, obeyed at least one divine commandment, and did their best to multiply and replenish the earth. So Tumblefold was always full of children, and children catch fevers quite easily. If they get better, well; if they die, it is also well, for they are assuredly better off. Besides, there is the insurance money.

Yet for the solemn starved eyes of the little ones there was one great joy. Standing against a wall at a high part of the Fold you could see stretching away a great dark mass of tiled and slated roofs; and beyond the furthermost, rising just above them, was a long line of tree tops.

Many and many the little ones who, with

ragged, dirty pinafores, have stood against that wall on summer nights, watching the green tops of the trees moving in the wind, and golden and splendid as the rays of the setting sun fell on them. To us, children then, they were thousands of miles away, and might almost be in that wonderful Heaven of which we heard so much from the lady who made weekly visits, with presents of tracts or picture texts, and whose lovely clothes had such a delicious smell.

There were pastimes, even there, usually played while sprawling on a dirty floor; for the little limbs were too weak to venture on the round, slippery stones which formed the pavement. We had fairy tales, too, and even rude nursery rhymes; the favourite being "Baa-baa Black Sheep," with mysterious emphasis on the Black. For it often happened on market days that a flock of sheep coming up Barn Street would rush suddenly helter-skelter down Tumblefold, to the intense terror of its smallest inhabitants.

The one game played most by the little ones was a very queer game indeed. It was called "Father and Mother." A lad of three or four years would play the father, a little girl the mother, another lad the policeman, and the others would be the children.

The father would go out to work, and the

mother would stay at home to tidy the house and mind the children. Suddenly the boy-father would come in, maybe wearing his father's old hat, brandishing a big stick, and evidently drunk. He would open the game with:

"Is my dinner ready?"

Girl-mother: "No, it ain't."

Boy-father: "Why ain't it?"

Girl-mother: "'Cos I ain't got no money to get it with, yer nasty, drunken dog, you. It's well to be you, indeed, off drinkin' an' flyin' yer kite, while me an' these poor kids got nothin' to eat in the house."

Then the boy-father thrashed her with the stick; he shouted, she screamed, never hitting back; and the children pretended to cry. The boy-policeman rushed in and, after a struggle, hauled the drunken father to the lock-up, and the last words in this queer game came from the girl-mother: "If I'd 'a known you was goin' to bring me to this, I'd never 'a married you, Jack."

That was all. Just a childish imitation of the words and deeds of their elders. In the child-mind there was no germ of thought of the right or wrong of it. That it might be or ought to be different never occurred to them. It was a matter quite in the eternal order of things, something to which they themselves

must look forward.   So in their childish way
they prepared for it.

•   •   [•]   [•]   [•]

School days began at five.

At the same time began our initiation into
domestic secrets and mysteries of ways without means.   Then also loomed in view our
great bogey, the School Board officer.

In infancy we had been terrified when heedless or fractious by threats of being fetched
away at night by the black bogey up the
chimney; a sentence sufficient to calm all dis-
turbance.   And I know one of those four
whose childish mind was so affected by this
threat that for years he could not look up a
chimney without a tremor.

The School Board officer was a real bogey.
He was a tall old man with white whiskers,
and wore the usual tall hat and frock coat with
shiny buttons.   We grew to know him well,
and his appearance in the Fold at any time
was the signal for a scattering of the clans.

He was a frequent visitor to Tumblefold.
Its denizens kept no servants; the children
served instead.   They cleaned house and went
on errands, and in the not uncommon confine-
ments were kept at home to mind the house.
Toothache was a good excuse for absence from
school, and some of us had it often.   A few

days later would come the dreaded pencil-tap at the door, and a stern, familiar voice would ask why that boy had not been to school? What time the wretched culprit would be screwed up under the table in a dreadful state of mind, fearing discovery, and, may be, decapitation.

The errand-going alone kept us boys on a perpetual trot. We dared not rebel, because on it depended our Saturday pennies of pocket money. Your poor man's larder is never complete or extensive, and it was no unusual thing to come from school and rush to the grocer's for a pen'north of treacle, half a pound of sugar, and an ounce of tea, or to wait without breakfast in a morning till the shop opened which sold bread in penny-worths. For the older children there were the visits to the pawn-shop on Monday morning with the family's Sunday clothes, on Tuesday with the washing, and day by day during the week with any odd article that would realise ninepence or a shilling. On Saturday they would be fetched back, if it had been a week of work.

Every Saturday night, when the street was filled with traffic, the public-houses noisy as hell itself, and Tumblefold uproarious and quarrelsome, there would be in one house or another a missing father. And in summer or winter there would be a child pilgrimage from public-house to public-house till he was found, and coaxed and entreated to come home.

Sometimes the children succeeded; sometimes were punched and blasphemed out of the place, and returned home, to sit up miserably round the relics of a fire, waiting for the unsteady, heavy feet, the fumbling of the latch, and the lurch into the house which were the signals for the children to go to bed. There they lay awake, listening to the angry quarrel; or crept to the head of the stairs ready to spring out if the words grew so loud as to herald blows. Ah, they were queer Saturday nights for the children in Tumblefold.

There were always quarrels going on, either in the old rookery of a public-house in the middle of the Fold, called the Spotted Dog, or in one or other of the adjoining houses.

Sometimes the quarrels were kept within closed doors, and the children gathered outside and tried to peer through the shutter chinks, listening to the blows, sometimes the crashing of furniture, and time after time on the dark, damp air the cry, always a woman's, "Don't, Jack! *Don't* hit me again, Jack."

Sometimes the disputants came outside, and in the centre of an excited crowd carried on their battle. Always the children jostled to the front, and listened with too ready ears to the imprecations between every word; taking it all in with terrible eagerness, and pondering day and night on what this word meant, why that was used, and what there could be in another unknown word to cause a woman to tear up a huge stone and hurl it desperately at her husband.

Saturday night was the late night for the bigger lads. When eleven o'clock came, and the Spotted Dog turned out its company, we were always present. There were fights, not one, but several, and your street-boy dearly loves a fight. Especially when, as here, it is waged in the dark by drunken men, over big, slippery stones. The coolest and strongest man is liable to slip and crack his head against a projecting stone, to lie helpless, maybe unconscious, while his foe kicks him in the ribs or his face till the spirit of fair play comes in and the kicker is pulled away. Compared with this schooling in the realities of life our other school experience was tame and dull. Yet, with the fear of the School Board man before our eyes, we stuck to it. We liked it at first. In the infant school they combined pleasure with instruction. Who would not remember his numbers in that immortal ditty,

> "One, two, three, four, five,
> Johnny caught a fish alive—
> Six, seven, eight, nine, ten,
> Johnny put it back again.
> Why did he let it go?
> 'Cause it bit his fingers so."

When we left the mixed school and entered the school labelled "Boys," our hearts sank within us. The master wielded a cane—a threepenny one. I know; for I once fetched him one, little guessing that it would first be tried on mine own hands.

The teachers boxed our ears sometimes when the master was not looking, for we were often in trouble and not always deservedly so. If a teacher sees a number of boys always together he guesses mischief; often incorrectly in our case.

The worst blow was when they set us home-lessons. This, being time taken out of our playtime, was theft. Potter proposed running away; Jones seconded. Ryder wanted to know where to. Potter did not know, and Jones looked thoughtful. The Treetops were mentioned, but as no one knew where they lay, we had to give it up and accept the infliction under protest.

So we resigned ourselves to the daily cramming of arithmetic, grammar, and geography as a tyrannous formality, useless then and thereafter, which we might as well endure with a good grace as a bad one. We had our playtime at night, and could talk and dream of the good days to come when we should leave school, go out to work, and in some way or other earn our own living.

Day by day we five went to school with slates on our backs and usually with a crust of bread and lard in our hands. We were always given the crusty end of the loaf, and were told that the eating thereof would make our hair curl. A deceit and a snare we unsuspiciously fell into, for we had a hankering for curls.

From the first we had a definite order of going and a fixed trot: Potter and I on the right, Ryder and Jones on the left. When Stubbs came we put him in the middle. From this we seldom varied. If we did, the Others, who had quickly marked our peculiar arrangement, and resented being left out, would obligingly put us right with the caustic cut that only your street-boy can use.

In school we were just the same. We held together like bricks in an old building. If by accident one of us dropped a marble on the floor, laughed during prayers or upset an ink-pot, no amount of threats would produce the faulty one. At last the master adopted a mean, unmanly device. Whenever he failed to get the actual offender, he called out Stubbs to be caned, and the terror in his face as he walked up always fetched out the right one before the cane descended.

But at night, when errands were finished, **we** were free. Potter called for Ryder, both **for** Jones and me, and altogether we went for

Stubbs; then with a peculiar shout of our own we proceeded to enjoy ourselves in ways and under conditions hereafter to be described.

CHAPTER IV

HOW FIVE LITTLE BOYS WENT SINGING CAROLS

WE stood together under a window in Tumblefold one foggy night, waiting for Jones, who was finishing his home-lessons. When he came he shouted out eagerly: "I say, it's only three weeks till Christmas."

We hailed the news with joyful surprise, although we had heard it in the same way, and at the same time, for at least a week.

"I hope it snows," said Jones.

"Why?" said Ryder, looking at his boots, which wanted mending.

"Why?" said Jones, " 'cause I shall go sweepin' the snow off the shop-fronts, and get some money for Chris'mus. I've saved none yet."

"Nor me," remarked Ryder ruefully.

Neither had Potter and I, but we did not say so. It was unnecessary.

"I've got a shillin' saved up," said Stubbs, proudly.

"You ought to," said Ryder. "Yer mother gives it yer. We have to work for ourn."

"I turn the mangle," said Freddy,. in extenuation.

"That ain't fetchin' hundred-weights o' coal, is it?" retorted Ryder.

"I tell you what," interposed Jones, eagerly; "I've been thinkin'——"

We turned round in surprise. Potter looked at him rather jealously. Thinking was *his* prerogative.

"I've been thinkin'," continued Jones. "I tell you what. Let's go singin' carols. We shall get lots o' money. We might get a Pound. Who knows?"

This was a good idea to all of us, excepting Potter.

"Who'll sing 'em?" said he, to Jones. "*You* can't sing. Teacher says your singin's howlin'——"

This was a nasty personal remark, and Jones promptly lost his temper.

"Look here, Potter, d'you want to fight?"

"I'll fight you, any day," said Potter, nonchalantly.

"All right," said Jones, spitting on his hands; "cock yer fisses up. I can lick you if your uncle is in the Rifles."

They were squaring off when we got between, and, after much noise and sundry threats on both sides, cooled them down.

Peace being restored, we spent that night talking the matter over in low voices, interrupted often by Potter with: "Sh! don't talk so loud. If some of the rough lot hear us it'll be all up."

The prospects were good. To our knowledge Tumblefold had heard no carol-singing before, and might turn out its pennies generously for such a novelty.

"Who knows any carols?" asked Potter, who had now assumed the leadership.

There was no reply. Our spirits drooped, till Freddy Stubbs said, "I've got a Carol Book."

"Why didn't yer say so before!" said Potter, savagely; "go an' fetch it, quick."

Stubbs ran, and was away a long time.

"Just our luck," said Potter, discontentedly; "he's lost it."

"No, he ain't," said Jones, excitedly, as Freddy came running back.

"Will you shut yer face?" asked the irascible Potter. "Don't want all the Fold to know, do yer?"

Freddy's arrival turned the dialogue. We could have hugged him as we stretched out our hands for just one look at the Carol Book.

"What shall we learn?" asked Potter.

" 'Christ is born,' " said Jones.

"Too hard," said Ryder. "Let's have 'While Shepherds.' "

" 'Sunny Banks' the easiest," suggested Stubbs.

We talked and talked, and at different times had selected each of the twenty old carols the book contained. We parted without settling anything. Potter stowed the Carol Book inside his vest. Stubbs looked hurt.

"It's all right, Freddy," said Potter, patronisingly, "you're too little, yer know. What should we do if somebody was to knock yer down an' pinch it?"

This was dreadful, and Freddy yielded at once.

Night after night went by. We met mysteriously, talked in whispers, hummed snatches of one carol and verses of another, and came no nearer to any conclusion.

Christmas Eve arrived, and found us arranging to meet on Christmas night, after tea, for the start. Our repertoire consisted of four verses of "While Shepherds Watched," nearly two verses of "Christ is Born," one verse of "The first Good Joy that Mary had," and the whole of "As I sat on a Sunny Bank." Besides these, we had the chorus. We *did* know that, and could sing it without a break.

Christmas night came. At half-past five four of us stood under our window. The absent one was Ryder. He came late, walking slowly, and his face was very white in the gaslight, while his fingers fumbled nervously with his bottom waistcoat button.

"I've been sick," he said, dejectedly. "I think it was the puddin'."

A sympathetic tremor went through our stomachs.

We stood there for five minutes. Our courage was gone, and we would have hailed with joy the first proposal to go home. It was warm indoors, and to-night we were a-cold.

Jones, however, being the author of the venture, meant trying it, and said regardless of grammar: "Look here, am we goin' or am we not?"

"Of course we're goin'," was the reluctant response.

"Come on, then," he said, assuming the leadership; "we'll go to Potter's first. I'll knock at the doors and Ryder'll hold the money."

We stood dubiously round the door.

"Now, then, Ryder," said Potter coaxingly, "start it."

"Can't," said Ryder, quickly. "Let Yeubrey start it. He sings better'n me."

I denied it, and was suggesting Stubbs, when Jones, in disgust, broke out violently:

"While—shep-eds watch their flocks-by-night."

One by one we joined it. At the end of the first verse we were all there. We began the next finely, then memory basely deserted us. Ryder fell first. At the end of the second verse Stubbs and I dropped out. Two more lines and Potter retired beaten. Jones fought against odds for another verse, then *he* hesitated and was just breaking down when he made a brave effort and rolled out:

"I wish you a merry Christmas,
I wish you a merry Christmas,
I wish you a merry, merry Christmas,
And a happy New Year."

We were with him in that, much to his relief. That effort saved us, and Jones was a hero among us for weeks after. Even Potter played second fiddle. Jones stuck to it bravely all night. He started the singing each time, sang every word he knew, and when we gave up incited us to keep putting in time to the refrain of *La, la, la, la, la.* The moment he felt his memory going he burst out vigorously:

"I wish you a merry Christmas."

Then, with a modest, virtuous expression on his face, he knocked at the door.

Fortunately for us the dwellers in Tumblefold knew nothing of music, and less of carols, so we went through our mutilated versions without detection.

The effect was great. Such a thing had never happened before in the Fold. They came to the doors, and stood listening as we went from house to house. With few exceptions, and they were very poor, each found some odd copper or coppers for us. Regardless of consequences they regaled us with thick slices of the inevitable plum-pudding till we grew mutinous. Being seasonably merry, they insisted on seeing us eat it, and twenty-four slices of plum-pudding are too much for any boy. But by many ingenious devices we managed to stow it away in pockets and sleeves, till each was a walking, clammy mass of pudding.

The youngsters came round in dozens, while the roughs chaffed us jealously from a distance. Potter, shorn of his leadership, fell to clearing away the children, alternately coaxing and bullying with—"Now then, you kids; why can't y' get off? Can't y' see we've got no room to breathe? How can we sing, if we've got no room to breathe, eh?"

This cleared them away for the space of two seconds and no more. So Potter gave up.

By the time we had finished the Fold we had taken three-and-fourpence in pennies, halfpennies, and one threepenny piece. Our joy was unlimited, and our progress was delayed by the frequency with which we made Ryder turn out his pockets to see that none was missing. Quite a dozen times the threepenny piece was lost, and all five breathlessly raked the coppers till it was found. At last our fears were so excited that we put Ryder in the middle, and formed a guard of four round him, for we feared footpads.

The Spotted Dog welcomed us uproariously. In some trepidation we filed between the tables and stood in front of the fire, in obedience to the company's order. They plied us with beer; some of it we drank, with consequent mixtures of vision and further losses of memory.

But we stuck to it firmly, Jones, of course, shining. We ran through our curious medley, in every moment of doubt commencing, "I wish you a merry Christmas," and finishing all together. Alas, we were hopelessly muddled, and at last each started his own carol in his own way. It must have sounded something like this:

> "While shepherds watched—a sunny bank,
> A sunny—flocks by night—
> The angel of the—Christ is born—
> A—and glory shined—on a sunny bank.
> —I wish you a merry Chris'mas
> A sunny b—erry Chris'mas,
> I wish you a merry Chris'mas,
> An' a happy—day in the morning."

The effect must have been prodigious, but

as we made up in sound what was lacking in sense, nobody was any the wiser, and the company clattered their jugs and thumped the tables till we sang it again.

"Gawd strike," was the general remark, "them kids can sing, though."

We listened with blushing modesty, though we did not doubt their word for a moment. They rose to the occasion, too, and collected one-and-eightpence for us. This brought our total to five shillings, a shilling each already! we were rich, and indulged in dreams of oranges and cokernuts on the morrow. Monkey nuts were off.

But gain begets gain, or the desire of it, and though we were tired and hoarse, we left the Fold and went on, having several likely places in view. Our experiences were less pleasant, however; doors were slammed in our faces, and policemen pursued us. One pleasant-faced man told us that if we went up a certain entry and sang at a certain door, the inmates would be sure to give us sixpence. We sang there for ten minutes before we found that it was a cow-house. Another old gentleman invited us into his kitchen, and laughed while we sang for half-an-hour; then he dismissed us with his blessing and—Twopence! This was mean, and when he had closed the door we kicked it fiercely, after whispering through the keyhole, "*You* skinny old monkey!"

We came to a coffee-house, and under its window counted up our cash. It came to five-and-tenpence, being one-and-twopence each. Ryder, whose weakness was soup, wanted to go in the coffee-house. But no, we had one more call to make and we meant making it. So we went on.

We arranged ourselves round the door, and were well under way when Jones stopped, open-mouthed and hair on end.

"I say—I say," he gasped, "where's Ryder?"

We looked round in alarm. He was gone.

"He's run off with the bloomin' money," shrieked Potter. "Come on—we'll have him."

We rushed away, heedless of the people of the house, who came to the door, surprised at our sudden stop. We sped through the streets, asking every policeman if he had seen a lad with pale face, dark hair, about our size, with his pockets full of money, our money, and without giving the paralysed officials time for answer were away again.

Once we chased an imaginary Ryder down an entry. We were punching him on the floor when a woman appeared, and laid about her vigorously. Then we fled, having pummelled the wrong boy. Through the streets again, then to Tumblefold, to see if he had gone home. But no Ryder was to be found.

"I know," said Potter; "he's gone to London. Let's go to the station and see."

We rushed there, to learn that no train had gone to London, and that five-and-tenpence would not take him there. Tired out, and nearly crying, we walked moodily homewards till we came to the aforementioned coffee-house. And lo, just coming out, wiping his wicked mouth, was Ryder.

We guessed it at once. It was soup.

Before he quite knew what had happened he was lying on his back, and we four were on top of him gabbling incoherently.

"Y'r bloomin' thief!—where's our money? —where's my one-and-tuppence?—he's spent it, the bloomin' Pig, he has—hold him tight, Jones—I've got him—ah, would yer?—fetch a Bobby—feel in his pockets—let's have him locked up—"

All the time Ryder was struggling and pleading piteously for mercy. At last, after we had nearly disembowelled him, we allowed him to sit up, two holding his arms, one clasping his neck, and Jones sitting on his legs.

"Now, then, y'r bloomin' thief, where's the money?"

Ryder was crying. "I ain't a thief," he said.

"Well, what did yer run away for?"

Then it came out. The thought of the soup had been too much for him, and after trying in vain to resist temptation, he yielded, and slipped off to spend his share, never dreaming that we should suspect him of theft. In fact, he reminded us of an agreement, which we in our excitement had forgotten, to meet afterwards and share our takings at this same coffee-house.

So he produced the money. While we were counting it, Ryder went suddenly white.

"Hello, what's up?" inquired Jones.

"I've spent fivepence out of my share," said Ryder, faintly.

"You spent fivepence already? You *have* got a bloomin' stummock, after all that puddin'. What 'ave you 'ad?"

"Soup," moaned the unfortunate, *"I had five basins,* and you sat on my stummock, yes, you did, oh-h-h!"

Ryder was ill. And what with remorse for our unjust suspicions, regret for the way we had pummelled him, and the shaking our own pudding-filled stomachs had received in pursuing him, we were nearly as ill. So, painfully and wearily we trudged arm-in-arm homewards, Ryder in the middle, gasping at intervals:

"Oh, dear, my stummock. It's the soup what did it; yes, it was."

We took him home, and dispersed. We met next day, and soon spent our hard-earned pocket-money. But, grown wise by experience, we never went carol singing again.

CHAPTER V

"LITTLE boy, will you go in that—that place, and ask if Mr. Neville is there? Say his—a lady wants him."

The little boy was Stubbs. "That place" was The Spotted Dog. Freddy willingly agreed, and trotted away. Meanwhile we surveyed the lady. She stood back in the shadows, as if afraid of being seen; a tall young woman, aged perhaps thirty, dressed plainly, with a worn Cashmere shawl thrown loosely over her shoulders. Her face had undoubtedly been handsome, but was now white and pinched, and showed the sharp lines of misery and suffering. In her eyes the far-seeing expectancy of youth had given place to an inscrutable introspective look, as of one who had learned a great secret, and could gain no rest from brooding on it.

She was a lady, a real lady. There was no doubt of that.

Her presence and her errand in Tumblefold caused no surprise. The Spotted Dog, being out of the way and invisible from the street, was notorious for miles round Wolverhampton as a resort for men who wished to indulge their drinking and gambling habits, secure from discovery by their wives and relatives.

Many of its customers were strangers to Tumblefold, and included men of all classes and conditions in life. The police seldom visited it, and never at night. Sometimes a man would visit it for the first time, well clad and cared for; he would begin spending his nights and sometimes his days there, till in a few months he would be a physical wreck and a social pest. Here boys of sixteen were taught the worst vices of their seniors; gambling was favoured by all, young or old; and in the spacious yard at the back cockfights and prizefights were not unknown.

Almost nightly some woman managed to trace her husband's whereabouts, and the scenes that occurred as the woman tried, sometimes in tears, sometimes with fierce words and blows, to get the man away, were terrible object-lessons to the few who cared to see. Sometimes there was a pitched battle, and if there is anything repulsive and dishonouring to humanity it is to see a man, half drunk and half mad, pitching his brute strength against the starved, desperate frame of the woman from whom a just God has decreed that no man shall sunder him.

Freddy was some minutes away. As he opened the door a roar of laughter came out behind him.

"Well," said the stranger, "is he there?"

"Yes," said Freddy, "says he'll come when he's ready."

"So," said she, with a curl of her lip, "I *have* found you, at least"—— "Thank you, little boy," to Stubbs, "I am very much obliged to you."

The words were cold enough, but there was something touching in the way she patted the lad's cheek with her worn white hand. The very action suggested that there had been a time when the touch of that hand was enough to bring hunger and yearning to a man's heart.

She did not go away. She stood in the darkness, just above The Spotted Dog, listening to each rowdy, rollicking chorus. When we turned indoors she was still there. That was Monday night.

The same thing happened the next night, and the next; indeed, every night that week. Each time Stubbs was the one spoken to, always with the same pleading voice and eyes. Each time he came back with some evasive reply, and received the same gentle touch on his cheek. This had its effect on Freddy, and one night he burst out:

"If he was my father, and she was my mother, I'd kill him. I would. I'd kill him dead."

This murderous outburst was so unusual from the gentle-hearted Freddy, that we forced an explanation. So he told us.

Mr. Neville, "Gentleman," as the men in The Spotted Dog called him, was a man of very stylish appearance, and flourished rings, watch-chain and scarf-pin. His face was blotched, and when he was nearly drunk was fiery red. He spent money freely, was always playing cards, and swore as neatly as though he had been educated in Tumblefold.

On this particular night he swore loudly at Freddy and his message; the others chaffed him about "his old woman," and asked him to "fetch her in." This excited his drunken vanity. Protesting that "she was a fine bit of flesh," he produced a portrait, taken just before marriage. This was handed round, and subjected to the obscene comments which only a mixed gang of half-drunken men of low tendencies can make. Freddy unwillingly repeated a few, and even to us, familiar as we were with the Tumblefold vocabulary, they were horrible. Freddy, however, did not tell her of this.

Saturday night came, but not the lady. Half-an-hour before closing time we were waiting outside the Dog for the fun of turning out, when she came hurriedly towards us.

"Be quick, dear," she said, "tell him he *must* come. *Now,* at once, tell him. Baby's very ill."

Freddy looked up, and caught the suspense in her eyes, then went in. He came out quickly, with the same devils' laughter behind him.

"Well," she said, as Freddy faltered.

"He says—and they say—if you want him you must go in yourself."

"They? Who are they?"

"Why, the other men—you know—what are drinking with him."

Her face grew hard, and her eyes bitter. And for the first time Freddy missed the now familiar touch on his cheek. She stood there in the cold and darkness; listening, as we listened, to the choruses that came from The Spotted Dog.

Low, vile songs they were; though well enough adapted to their singers. Maudlin music-hall ditties with la-la-la refrains, about jolly boys, and darling girls, and sticking together, and fighting for Brave Old England. Every chorus finished with stamping of feet, rattling of jugs, and a roar of laughter, shouts, and oaths.

Then a man's voice rang out, harsh and weak at first, till long practice mastered the effects of drink, and the song was finished in a strong, rich voice. The voice was a strange one, so was the song. It was "Annie Laurie." Who was the singer? The woman knew.

"And for bonnie Annie Laurie
I'd lay me down and dee."

Her lips curled as she heard it. "Would to God you had," she said, "it would have been better for us both."

She turned to us, who stood near her. "That was my husband," she said, as if longing to unburden herself; "he was very ill once, and we thought he was dying. And one night, just before the change, he asked me to sing, and I sang that. And it has been his favourite ever since."

There was just a touch of pride in her voice.

The clock struck eleven. The lights were turned out, and the reeling, vomiting, cursing mob came out into the Fold. It was very dark, and freezing hard.

Gentleman was in the midst of an admiring group, all more or less drunk. But his wife walked straight to where he stood.

"At last," she said.

"It's all right, m' love," he said, with a

maudlin leer; "can't leave good company all
at once, y' know."

An angry retort was on her lips, but at the
moment one of the others stepped forward
familiarly with outstretched hand.

"Shake hands, missis, we wanted to see you.
You was a fine young woman when you was
married, you was," admiringly. "I've seen yer
portrait."

"You?" she said, witheringly, thrusting
down his hand. "When? Where?"

"Las' night, in the Dog," said the man, quite
hurt by her tone; "he showed it round to the
company," nodding towards Gentleman.

She turned to him, white and wild. "Is
that true, George? *You did that?*"

He saw her face, and like a coward was
silent. Then he saw steal on her face another
expression, that death, yea, even eternity,
would never efface; the look of a woman who
by the one nearest of all others to her has
been led out into the street, stripped, and
handed over to a mob of brutes for promis-
cuous violation.

That was what it meant to her. He could
see it working in her face, as she pictured to
herself the whole scene, the indescribable
words and the indescribable looks and thoughts
of the men who had bandied her portrait about.
She felt it all, helpless, hating, and loathing,

and knew that never again in life or in death would her body feel pure and clean.

And he saw it all, as the light of one flickering gas jet fell on her face. Then, seeing what he had done, knowing himself to be guilty of the foulest crime a man can commit against a woman, with no excuse and no possible extenuation, in craven fear he struck her full in the face—just to hide that look.

She fell against the wall. It was a hard blow, and drew blood, but she never even moaned. Blows were merciful in comparison with what he had already done.

But others resented the blow. For a common labourer to thrash his wife was a pastime, but this woman was so evidently a lady, and withal so friendless and helpless, that there were angry shouts at once.

The man who had spoken to her laid his heavy hand on Gentleman's arm.

"You're a coward," he said, "you're a dirty dog, to hit the woman like that."

Gentleman's response was to strike at him —and miss. The other's fist caught him under the jaw, and felled him.

"Fight it out," was the general shout. "Let 'em have it out, now."

A ring was quickly formed, and the two set in the middle. There was a look on Gentleman's face which meant mischief.

His wife was with a few women whose sympathies had gone out to her. They washed the blood from her face, and spoke kindly, if coarsely, to her. She said very little, and watched the fight without a sign of emotion. The man was dead to her.

It was a terrible fight; the worst we had ever seen. The labourer was a man of huge strength, but what Gentleman lacked in strength he made up in skill and dexterity. It was plain before many blows had been struck that he was a clever boxer. They fought on, slipping and stumbling over the hard stones, but keeping their feet well, considering.

The onlookers were in transports, and jostled and pushed to get a good view. They kept the ring clear, and shouted encouragingly to both fighters, though the labourer was the favourite.

They fought for half-an-hour. Their clothes were torn, and their faces covered with blood, but they stuck doggedly to it. It was noticed that the labourer was getting tired.

"It's a Beautiful fight," shrieked an onlooker, "stick to it, lads."

A sinister glare came into Gentleman's eyes as he saw the other's weakness, and he swung out suddenly to end the fight, but his foot slipped for the first time, and he pitched to the ground, striking full with his forehead a projecting stone. The labourer was on him at once, but was pulled off.

"Get up, Gentleman," was the cry, "have it out, now."

Gentleman did not reply—did not even move. In turning him over they found a hole in his forehead, from which blood was flowing. And at that moment the police came up. Seeing the seriousness of the case they staunched and bathed the wound, and fetched a cab. Then, with the labourer in custody, Gentleman, and his wife, they drove to the Hospital, leaving Tumblefold speechless with excitement. It was noticed that the woman, after the first look in his face as he lay on the ground, never touched, even with her fingertip, her husband.

The doctors closed round him as the policemen laid him down. One look was sufficient. After a whisper one of them advanced, and said to her:

"Are you his wife?"

She just bent her head.

"I am very sorry, ma'am," said the doctor, "but—he's dead."

She looked at him strangely.

"Yes, yes, I know," she said wearily; "he died—*when was it?*" turned suddenly to the labourer.

The man stared blankly, then met her eyes, and spoke quickly:

"Last night it was, about ten o'clock."

"That he died?" she said.

"That he died," said the man, in awe.

The doctors looked puzzled.

But the labourer knew.

CHAPTER VI

IN SUMMER DAYS

AS we grew older the coming of the summer was a pleasure we began to look forward to as soon as Christmas was past. Every winter seemed to be harder and harder than the last, and the gaunt skeleton, whose shadow was always over Tumblefold, seemed drawing nearer and nearer; so near at last that it needed little imagination to see the sleepless horror entering house after house without knocking or warning.

In summer the burden was a little, just a little, more bearable. If the house held no food the hunger-pang was not so biting as in winter. The sunlight, too, as it slowly went round the Fold during the day, was pleasant for the little ones to play in.

On hot nights, when every stone in the pavement, and even the bricks in the walls, seemed hot, and the darkness was reluctant to dispel the all-exposing light, the women came out and sat each on her own doorstep. They talked and laughed there till far into midnight, while in excited parties the children played till even they were too tired to do anything but lie down in whispering, weary heaps under the walls.

Every week there was usually some fête and gala in the town. Every balloon which ascended was visible in the Fold, and passed, almost in mockery, right over the great labyrinth of misery; while with open mouths and upturned eyes the ignorant Folders watched the graceful marvel pass out of sight. Then they settled down to wait for the fire-works. Those visible were usually fire-balloons, rockets, and serpents. To the excited eyes of the watchers the brilliant colours and transformations as rocket after rocket whizzed up and burst were uncanny and almost miraculous.

To the women, or most of them, the summer brought holidays. Hardly a week passed but a party of half-a-dozen, or more, set forth on an annual journey to various places, all having one occupation, pea-picking, in view. Some of the older hands, who were respected accordingly, went hop-picking, miles and miles away. They took train to their resort, having scraped and saved for weeks or pawned to get the necessary fares.

In a few weeks each party returned with health and sunburns enough to last twelve months; and for the space of a week, or less, there would be plenty, if not always peace, in each house, including tinned salmon for tea and unlimited beer and mussels for supper.

To us in particular, summer was a grand time. Our playtime was prolonged, our stomachs were less troublesome, and it was not so necessary in making our plans to consider the condition of our clothes or boots. If our boots were very bad, we could do without them. There was no pride about us.

Our amusements were infinite. Running, tipcat, toys, marbles, and even a rude form of cricket; the wickets being three long chalk marks down a suitable wall, and the batsman being declared out if the ball showed the white mark which betrayed contact with the wickets.

There was fun at night, when the whole Fold was at its door breathing the air, heavy and vile, yet life-giving compared with that in the houses. Even the rain brought its pleasures. If the storm were heavy, the sewers were stopped up, and a dirty rivulet ran down the main gutter. In this we sailed paper boats, bits of wood, and even match stalks, tracing breathlessly their passage down to the wide estuary which marked the flooded sewer.

The road from which the Fold branched was the old main road, leading one way right through the Black Country, and the other leading through Shropshire into Wales. There were many pretty villages and pleasure resorts on this road, and every morning excursions numbering from six to twenty brake loads each rolled down it from all parts, seeking fresh air and ale in the green country. Late at night they came back, the weary horses climbing the long hill, unheeded by their load of young and old; the old sitting cheek by jowl, and the young in assorted couples clasping each other's waist; all joining sleepily in the chorus of some old hymn or popular ditty. They never cared which, so long as they knew the chorus. The children of Tumblefold used to run in dozens behind these brakes, clamouring for the pennies and flowers which were not seldom thrown among them.

Long-looked for and prayed for but never hastening on that account, came the breaking-up of school for the midsummer holidays. For three whole weeks our time was our own, and school-lessons and home-lessons were consigned to brief oblivion.

We were free. Free, that is, providing that errands were done and house duties performed; that our clothes and boots were in sufficient repair to justify risk, and that none was down with fever. .

We five at an early age took a dislike to Tumblefold by daylight. On all possible occasions we left it behind us, seeking the first green field or patch of grass we could find in preference to the familiar old town. Time could not tell of the journeys after birds' nests we never found, the expeditions after fish we never caught, and the long lounges under hedges in country lanes, talking and dreaming. Always we returned with bunches of wild flowers, which were lovingly placed in broken jugs in the windows, and remained there till others replaced the dead and withered remnants.

This was always our holiday programme. It was cheap, costing nothing but bootleather; and as we took our slices of bread and lard, or dripping, wrapped up in our pockets, seldom returning before night, it usually saved a dinner.

One summer the usual tramps were commenced, but being now somewhat familiar with them, we grew tired, with boyish love of change. And Potter had an idea: "I'll tell you what," he said. "Let's have a big walk. Let's walk to London."

We were staggered.

"London!" said Ryder, scornfully; "who are yer havin'? It's over a hundred miles. It's too far."

"Who says it's too far?" retorted Potter, nettled; "we can walk it there an' back in a day."

We agreed, hopefully. It seemed quite feasible, for our ideas of distance were crude and boyish. Indeed, our two-mile tramps, with several hours lying down at the finish, were talked of among ourselves as twenty-mile walks.

So we decided to walk to London the very next Sunday morning, and fully expected to get back by nightfall. None of us, not even Potter, knew which road led to London, but Ryder had a sister in service at a village ten miles away, and we concluded that that must be the road.

Sunday morning came. Saying nothing of our purpose we set forth, deciding as we started to call and see Ryder's sister. Keeping step, and walking in the middle of the road, we went on briskly for a mile. We were then out of the town. It was a new road to us; straight and clean, with hedges and fields on each side of it.

"It's grand," said Jones, sniffing the fresh air and stepping out; "I could walk like this for a week."

"So could I," said Ryder, with a grin of satisfaction.

Potter glowed with joy at the success of his suggestion. Stubbs and I said nothing—we were walking.

It was one of the few perfect days in an

English summer. The sun was not too hot as yet, the skies were smokeless and blue, and the air around and above us seemed full of the song of birds.

Our spirits rose, and we talked gaily of the story we should have to tell on returning. The second milestone was passed, and the third, and the fourth. Then we came to a little village. A policeman was walking towards us. As we met him Potter asked with an air of importance, "Please, sir, how many miles is it to London?"

The policeman eyed us up and down with stolid face, then unexpectedly lashed out with his cane, exclaiming: "Hook it, yer cheeky little varmints, hook it."

We hooked it. Stubbs, as usual, the least wary, caught the blow, and came running after us, crying.

"Serves you right," said Potter, unfeelingly, "why didn't you look out?"

We went on. In a few minutes the sun became hot, then very hot. We took off our coats and stuck to it, sweating greatly. But our footsteps slackened, and when we came to milestone number nine we stopped dead.

"Come on," shouted Potter, "we shan't get there to-day."

As he showed no inclination to go on, we stood as we were, very hot and very tired.

Nine miles, and ninety-one at least to go! still it did not sound so *very* bad.

"Come on," said Ryder, "it's only a mile to my sister's. We'll have a rest there. She's sure to give us some cake. I know where it is."

Growing wearier at every step, we went on, till we came to the village. Then we discovered that Ryder had no idea where his sister lived, and vilified him accordingly. After an hour's trudging we found the house, and knocked at the door. Her astonishment at seeing us was great, but was greater when Potter told her in his matter-of-fact way that we were walking to London.

She laughed loudly, and called to her fellow-domestics.

"I say, girl-l-ls, here's five little kids walkin' all the way to London!"

They joined in the laugh, while we looked severely at Ryder, as if he were responsible for his sister's bad manners.

She was a good-natured girl, and the master and mistress were out. So she regaled us with cake and bread and butter and gave each a glass of beer. We sat there for nearly an hour.

Then Potter got up. "We must start," he said sternly, "it's a long way yet."

Ryder's sister was looking at him. He stood

up for about two seconds, then plumped back in his seat. He was tired. It could hardly have been the ale. Strange to say, on getting up, we all did exactly the same. What with being tired and stiff, to say nothing of the beer, we were in a funny condition.

Miss Ryder was jubilant. It was the only diversion she had had for weeks. "Look here, lads," she said, "you must walk home now. Go to London some other day. It's too late; you won't get there before night; then where will you sleep?"

She kept us there till late in the afternoon, then started us off with cake in our pockets and a huge bunch of flowers to divide when we reached home.

We stepped out merrily homewards. We went on grandly for two short miles. Then Jones found a nail in his boot and Freddy said he could not walk another inch. We sat down and rested. We were worse when we stood up. We were all in a pitiful condition, and had eight miles to go.

. . . . .

Late that night, when all Tumblefold was in excitement over the strange disappearance of five little boys who had never before missed their Sunday dinners, those same little boys staggered and limped down from the street in such a miserable state that even the threatened thrashings were mercifully withheld. So were the suppers, and we climbed painfully to bed.

But we never finished that walk to London.

CHAPTER VII

ON WINTER NIGHTS

IN spite of its disadvantages, we liked the winter better than summer. Not that we did not feel its pinches on days when a dirty, drenching rain soaked through our patched rags and dilapidated boots; or on nights of keen frost when we were outside running and jumping ourselves into warmth while our elders were indoors shivering over scanty fires.

Besides, being obliged to double our exercise just to keep warm, our appetites increased and were never fairly satisfied. We bore it patiently, having sure and certain hopes of a good time coming. For the shortening of the days betokened the approach of the happiest time of the year, when for a whole week we fared in what seemed to us to be a royal fashion; on roast beef, plum pudding, mince pies and nuts. Yea, sometimes, if work had been very good, or there had been a bit of luck in a raffle, sometimes on goose. How we counted the weeks and the days till Christmas came!

There were other reasons why we liked the

dark nights. The all-revealing summer sun fell unsparingly on Tumblefold; lit up its darkest passages, and betrayed its dirt and squalor and degradation to all who passed through. It was not pleasant in our sight. But the darkness invested the labyrinthine medley of warrens and burrows with an air impressive and mysterious. The memories of three hundred years of eventful, endless change rose like an exhalation from its old basements and filled the Fold, till the light came, with solemn, sombre glamour.

To us boys it was a wonder, aye, a marvel, by night. We played in and about its darkest alleys, and had dozens of hiding-places whence we defied parental control. There were nights when we sallied into the street and irritated the policeman on duty till he chased us savagely down the Fold; striding into the darkness only to hear around and behind him derisive yells as we ran in and out of our hiding-places.

There were places which we dared not pass singly, even in daylight. In the middle of the Fold, where the alleys were most intricate and misleading, was a great disused malthouse. It was bounded at one end by a long, narrow court, irregular as the building, which served as the neck of the system. This was Irish Row, notorious for fights and for at least one murder.

We passed through Irish Row every day to and from school. We held close together as we neared the malthouse. The shutter of one window had fallen down, revealing a bare, tiled floor, black with dust. Across this we used to stare till in the darkness at the end of the long room we could see hanging from the cobweb-shrouded beam the indistinct shape of a man; a man who many, many years ago had been found there one morning, dead.

.   .   .   .   .

Our games were many and various. Some were original, if nothing else. One such was called "Bees," and had a certain suggestive application. It was an ancient tradition that this game should be played with every new-comer into the Fold.

A dozen lads would place the innocent stranger against a certain wall, instructing him that he was to play the drone in the bee-hive and they the busy bees. He uttered the command, "Bees, bees, bring me honey." On this, flapping their arms in imitation of wings, puffing out cheeks and humming loudly, the bees fled away in pursuit of honey—to a tap round the corner where they filled their mouths with water. Then with cheeks dis-tended and still humming, they returned in a body and spurted the water over the unsuspecting drone, who was usually too much astonished to resent the joke.

We had various modifications of hide-and-seek, adapted to the peculiarities of the Fold; and the usual running and jumping games. For such intricate points as to who should set the first back or play blind man, there was always one formula to be observed. This was Finger-in-the-Pie. A hat would be produced: each lad would place a finger therein. With the words, "Last man in," the speaker would go round the fingers with his, touching a finger to each syllable of this mysterious jargon:

"Awkum, bawkum, booney kawkum,
Merikermeriker buzz;
In spin, on spon,
Ackerbo, ackerbo, twenty-one."

At "one" the finger touched fell out. Then it began again: the last one in paying the penalty.

One peculiar but popular game was Woody-woody-Woodcake. The principal stationed himself against the wall facing the main passage; the others hid themselves within earshot. His part was to ask certain questions, those in hiding answering. The dialogue was something like this, the fun was mostly in the shouting.

"Had yer breakfast?"

"Yes."

"Had yer dinner?"

"Yes."

"Blacked yer boots?"

"Yes."

"Washed yer faces?"

"Yes."

"Done yer home lessons?"

"Yes."

"Took yer father's dinner?"

"Yes."

"Run all yer errands?"

"Yes."

At this point the interlocutor was usually stumped and pronounced the magic sentence, *"Woody-Woody-Woodcake."* On which the members of the hidden chorus rushed from their places to the wall, the last to touch it with both hands paying the penalty by acting as questioner next time.

When the frost had fairly set in we were in high spirits. Though Tumblefold had neither lake nor pond, its gutters were always full, and we examined the longest every morning to see if it would bear, with an interest deeper than any country squire could take in his private lakelet. If in condition a noisy shout announced the fact, and we at once made a slide from top to bottom, down which, in our own phraseology, we "slithered."

When in full swing no words could express the yells of joy as first one and then another fell, and the next behind tumbled screaming on top of them. There was an element of danger, too, to give it spice. At the gutter's end was a sewer-grating, lacking two of its bars, and it needed great care to miss getting a foot down the grating. This happened sometimes, and always caused excitement; for the hole was wide enough to hold an ordinary boy's boot, and keep it there. So the unfortunate one had to hold still, while we unlaced his boot. When his foot was freed came the task of rescuing the boot. On one occasion it fell to the bottom of the sewer, and was not recovered for days. And the thrashing the unlucky loser received stopped our "slithering" for that night, at least.

Sometimes, by way of a change, we joined games with the girls, and subdued our rougher tendencies to theirs. What their games lacked in physical exercise was made up in variety and originality, to say nothing of the rhymes and musical effect. They had a quaint jingle, and a quainter tune to every game, and the effect, as in a band of thirty or forty we went dancing and chanting through the Fold in the darkness, must have been weird indeed to strangers. But few strangers ventured through at night.

Their favourite games were usually variations of dancing hand-in-hand in a circle. Kiss-in-the-ring was one, but here, as elsewhere, kissing went by favour, and the game often ended in strife and sore heads. We loved those games on winter nights. Rude, crude, and maybe coarse some of them were; but we entered into them with a half-prophetic zest, a zest that in a few years would be gone for ever.

Often in fancy I go back to those old times. I tread the intricate winding ways in the darkness, possessed by the old fear of falling into walls; I hear all around me the merry cries and shrill voices raised in song, and as in recognition I look into dozens of happy, pinched faces the bitterest thoughts come to me, as I pick out, slowly and sadly, one by one, the faces that have gone from Tumblefold for ever. For the children died young in Tumblefold. And they knew it, too. This is one of their songs:

"Wall flowers, wall flowers, growing up so high,
We are all little folks, and we shall all die;
Excepting Mary Wilkinson, and she's the youngest child,
Fie, for shame, fie, for shame,
Turn your back towards the game."

Another game went to the air of Yankee Doodle, and these words:

"Little Johnny's sick in be-ed,
What shall I send him?
Three good wishes,
Three good kisses,
And a slice of gingerbread."

The quaintest game was also the favourite. It had no particular name. The oldest girl usually played the mother, and the other children, joining hands, in a straight line danced backward and forward in front of her. They sang, to a very old air, their questions, repeating each three times, and finishing with "On a cold and frosty morning."

This, as nearly as I can remember it, is the jingle:

"Children: Mother, buy me a milkin' can,
Mother, buy me a milkin' can,
Mother, buy me a milkin' can,
On a cold and frosty mornin'.
Mother: Where's the money to buy it with?
Where's the money to buy it with?
Where's the money to buy it with?
On a cold and frosty mornin'.
Children: Sell my father's feather bed,
On a cold and frosty morning.
Mother: Where will y'r father lie
On a cold and frosty morning?
Children: Lie in the boys' bed
On a cold and frosty morning.
Mother: Where will the boys lie
On a cold and frosty morning?

Children: Lie in the girls' bed
On a cold and frosty morning.
Mother: Where will the girls lie
On a cold and frosty morning?
Children: Lie in the servant's bed
On a cold and frosty morning.
Mother: Where will the servant lie
On a cold and frosty morning?
Children: Lie in the pigstye
On a cold and frosty morning.
Mother: Where will the pig lie
On a cold and frosty morning?
Children: Lie in the *maiding tub
On a cold and frosty morning.
Mother: What shall I wash in
On a cold and frosty morning?
. Children: Wash in y'r thimble
On a cold and frosty morning.
Mother: What shall I sew with
On a cold and frosty morning?
Children: Sew with the poker
On a cold and frosty morning.
Mother: What'll I poke the fire with
On a cold and frosty morning?
Children: Poke it with y'r finger
On a cold and frosty morning.
Mother: Suppose I burn my fingers
On a cold and frosty morning?

Then the children broke loose, shouting, "Serve you right, serve you right," and the mother ran angrily amongst them, inflicting punishment.

Our playground, like our pastimes, was movable. If a neighbour's husband lay drunk

*Washing tub.

or asleep, we moved elsewhere. If a playmate were ill we moved also, and of our own accord. That was the shadow on our games; there was always some face missing. In time of fever it might be a dozen, and those who remained would look at each other in white fear as they met.

There was one little girl who was a favourite with us. A quiet, pale-faced girl, with eyes looking always inwardly. She was the best of us all. Her face and pinafore were always clean, and her frock when torn was neatly mended. She used to get the little ones round her, telling them stories or reading from her schoolbooks.

We five fell in love with her. She returned the feeling and loved us, not individually, but collectively. Our devotion grew so strong that we took turns to spend our pennies in peppermints for her. She always shared them.

One night she was missing from the girls' games. Next day it was whispered that she had the fever. A week later we stood by her door, waiting with white faces for the coffin to be brought out.

The children shed no tears. She was a gentle, lovable child, and a favourite with all. But others had gone before her. One by one, all that morning, we had crept slowly, with hushed lips and bare heads, up the ricketty stairs, to see her for the last time as she lay in her coffin. And on the face of the child, who lay with closed eyes and folded hands, was the same look of eternal peace we had seen brooding on the faces of the others gone before.

CHAPTER VIII

THE CURSE THAT FELL

STILL to this day the story is whispered in Tumblefold, and many a brawling blasphemer has bitten a flying oath with his teeth at the warning from a woman.

"Remember what happened to Champion Rew."

Champion was his common name, Rew was his Christian name in short; what his surname might be nobody knew or cared to inquire. He abhorred inquisitive people, and had a way of letting blows follow swiftly on resentment. The word his enemies used when speaking of him is unprintable here.

Even his friends were compelled at times to admit candidly, but guardedly, that he was good enough for anything, from pitch-and-toss to manslaughter.

He was a long, loose-limbed, big-boned fellow of thirty; when sober his face was

sneeringly sullen, when drunk it was satanic-
ally savage. He lived in periodical impulses,
and every impulse spent itself. As was once
said reflectively over the bar of the Spotted
Dog by a man he had thrashed a few minutes
before: "When he works he works, when he
drinks he drinks, and when he fights he fights
—by God, he does!"

When sober, however, he was comparatively
harmless, and had been known to work six
days at a stretch without going over the mark.
But when he was drunk he was not good company, and fights were always imminent. In
his youth he had been a champion middle-
weight boxer, and the old battle instinct had
not left him. Whenever possible, he fought
in the street, and with men—policemen for
preference. Failing them he staggered home,
and took it out of Lettie.

Lettie was a tall, thin woman of about his
own age. When first they came together she
was a robust, merry girl, utterly unlike him,
and why she should have taken up with him
none could understand. It was not that she
wanted a home, for she could earn twelve
shillings a week easily in a factory.

The neighbours spoke of her to the parson
and the district visitors as Mrs. Rew, and
lamented the trouble she had with Mr. Rew.
But amongst themselves or in her presence

they used her maiden name, and referred to
Rew as Lettie's man. So strangers tried
vainly to guess their relations to each other.
She wore no wedding ring, true, but that
might easily have been pawned. The only
cause for suspicion came when these same
neighbours quarrelled with Lettie, and referred to her children in terms which ques-
tioned their legitimacy in the eyes of the law,
and inferred that their pedigree was like their
mother's Sunday dress, a pledge unredeemed
and lost.

And for some reason or other the two did
not get on well together. After the first year
of their union they quarrelled continually.
Time after time Rew came home drunk, or
sober after losing all night at "ha'penny
nap," and vented his superfluous strength on
Lettie.

At first she bore it quietly and dragged her
bruised limbs and discoloured features to and
from work. But as child after child was born,
and her periods of absence from work grew
longer, she grew mutinous and defiant. And
when he staggered home with empty pockets,
as the result of his week's work, she—for the
sake of her children, not for her own—turned
on him and they quarrelled. She gave blow
for blow, till her little strength was gone, and
even then she cursed him with her eyes as he

held her to the ground with his knees and
pounded her face with his fists as we boys used
to pound bricks to dust with hammers when
our throstles and linnets needed fresh sand in
their cages.

Tumblefold was notorious for its fights,
but the worst of its quarrels were mere parlour
discussions to those which took place between
Champion Rew and Lettie.

They always quarrelled with closed doors,
shouting, screaming at each other; and the
children, of whom I was one, crowded on the
doorstep and peered through the chinks of the
shutters, while the neighbours stood some distance away listening to the crashing of furniture and the fearful oaths of the man.

When drunk he proved himself to be of a
highly sensitive nervous temperament, and he
had been known to suddenly fling open the
door and look down the Fold at the crowd in
the gully which formed the neck of Irish Row.
Then he uttered his worst oath, rushed fiercely
down the Fold, and charged into and scattered
the crowd.   And the man who could do that
was none of your scavengers, as Rew himself
declared, but a fighter and a Blue-splashed
Man.

But his oaths were so monstrous in their
blasphemy that even men heard them with a
shudder, while some of the women stopped

their ears with their fingers or screamed, for they were superstitious, these women. In things of this world they had no fear, but when everything, living or dead, in the invisible universe was invoked and cursed in a breath they shuddered and looked skywards for judgment.

There was one oath which the children knew by heart. It was his last oath, and no sooner was it spoken than the fight began. And the women said as they heard it, "Thee'lt dare it once too of'n, Rew, lad, once too of'n, one o' these days."

And yet, ill-used, kicked, bitten and starved as she was by this man, Lettie disdained the advice of all who knew her story and she would not leave him. "He'll kill thee one o' these days," she was often told; but she only looked suddenly in front of her and said nothing.

Sometimes, but only in the hope that it might change him, she allowed the police to take him. Hard labour was always the result, and however long the sentence might be, always waiting at the gaol gates with food and clothing for her man when he came out, was Lettie. And sometimes she even fought with the police who were dragging him away, as men drag a hound from the throat of a meaner brute.

She was a puzzle. What were her feelings

towards the man? It may have been love, of a solemn, sombre kind. And maybe that was a wise woman who said, "Women are never grateful except when they are ill-treated. Mercury gave them, amongst other gifts, a dog's heart."

And so in this fashion these two kept company in the ditch which runs along life's highway.

On Sunday nights during the summer Tumblefold was visited by a band of Brothers and Sisters from a chapel not far away, who came with hymn-books and a portable American organ to remind the denizens of the Fold that in their Father's house were many mansions; mansions different from those in Tumblefold; mansions whose wall papers were not peeling through damp; mansions with a little more furniture than an old bacon box and a couple of stools; whose paneless windows were not stopped up with dirty rags and bags of straw, and in front of which ran no germ-exhaling gutters.

The men wore tall hats and cuffs, and were suspected accordingly. But the women were respected, and as the younger girls came hesitatingly round with hymn-books in their hands they were received gently, if silently, and woe betide the man who should dare to say a coarse word to them.

The long prayers of the men were tolerated, and the occasional hints at the depravity of Tumblefold were received with stoical unconcern by the crowd of women, with shadowed eyes, who stood behind the crowd of dirty, eager children pressing round the "moosic."

For it was the music that made them silent, and caused them to talk in whispers long after the mission folk had gone away. Most of these women had learned in their childhood the hymns which were sung, and a long-forgotten strain of melody may bring tears to eyes that have grown hardened through years of the buffetings and brutalities of life.

And so, as the strains of "There's a Beautiful Land on High" beat softly against the grimy walls of the houses, the audience grew hushed and wide-eyed, and the laughter ceased in the smoke-room of the Spotted Dog.

The preacher looked on the faces before him, and swelled unconsciously in the pride of his mission. The young girls, to whom these visits to Tumblefold were as visits to the Bottomless Pit, looked in the white faces of the children, and in a moment, as it seemed, saw the same faces transfigured in a broader, sunnier square. The women of the Fold, with expressionless eyes fixed in front of them, had gone the longest of all journeys—back into innocent childhood. And the children, as they turned over the words "a beautiful land on high," thought of the tree tops, and decided that this land must lie behind them. It might still be a "land on high," for the tree tops were very high, as high as a "great big mountain," the little ones were told. As to what manner of land it might be they just wondered and wondered. They were sure of one thing. It was nothing like Tumblefold.

The result was always the same. The missioners went away discouraged and disheartened by the apparently unresponsive faces, and the terrible apathy of them all—and when they were gone the women crept into their dens, and the children huddled together under walls humming snatches of the tunes they had heard.

. . . . .

One Sunday night, the last in August, the usual meeting was being held. It had been hot and oppressive all day, and the smells were rising from the gutter, and it was clear that a storm was nearing.

The last hymn was being sung when a sudden yell caused the visitors to look round in surprise which changed to fear.

Champion Rew was careering down the Fold towards the meeting.

\ Champion was drunk. His headlong lurches showed that.

/ Champion was angry. His language proved that.

⎰ Champion had been fighting. One eye was closed in a sardonic grin. His face was smeared in blood, his own blood, as was testified by the blotch on the coat-sleeve with which he had wiped it. The skin was off his knuckles; he had been punching some one's face. But his trousers were torn and dirty at the knees. Champion had been floored; and behind, from top to bottom, he was covered with mud. Champion had been on his back in the gutter.

Furthermore, he had been "bested," or "worsted." The scorching rage in his blood-shot eyes showed that.

Right in the midst of the meeting he fell. The visitors recoiled with a shudder.

The preacher touched his sleeve, and was at once struck. Champion had seen Lettie in the crowd and was upon her.

His oaths are indicated by numbers.

"You (one, two, three). You (four, five), sarm singin' (six), you. What yer doin' eer, eh? Ger in the (seven, eight) house, yer (nine, ten, eleven), before I (twelve) cut yer (thirteen, fourteen) eye out."

Her face was scarlet with shame. This had never before happened on a Sunday night, and as she caught the pitying horror in the eyes of the women the despair of hell came into her eyes. It stayed there but a second; a blow from Rew's fist closed them, and stretched her on the ground. Without a word she picked herself up, and walked into her house. He followed her, chuckling savagely, and slammed the door. The children, who had rushed behind, heard him drag the table against the door.

The missioners went away with appalled faces. The men came to the door of the Spotted Dog. The women stood in a crowd against the wall which faced Rew's door. The children were crowded *against* that door. And all ears were listening.

A dead weight of darkness fell upon the Fold silently. There was terror in the darkness, and as Rew and Lettie yelled and screamed at each other, the women cowered as if the oaths were missiles striking against them.

It was a fearful quarrel. Lettie was more defiant than she had ever been, and screamed back at the man's curses with a hate intensified by her recent humiliation. The oil lamp in the kitchen was lit, but the darkness pressed against the faces of the children on the doorstep as if striving to push them away, though vainly. Suddenly the rain began to fall heavily, every drop with the weight of a stone. Then came a peal of thunder and a flash of lightning, which revealed the children still on the doorstep.

As if striving to outrave the storm they continued. Suddenly was heard a rush, a triumphant "I've got yer," and the sickening sound of a woman's head battering against a wall. This was followed by a startled yell, a backward stagger over a chair and a furious cry as something heavy, perhaps a stool, whizzed against the door. Lettie had thrown it. Then came his last oath. "So that's yer game. Now I'll rip yer blue-splashed white liver out—if I don't may God strike me blind, speechless, and parralettic this minnit!"

He was heard to rush towards her; then as he finished the words came a fearful flash of lightning, which smote aslant the Fold like the great Sword of God himself. In the same instant was heard a crash in Rew's house, a cry which struck down hellwards, then silence, and darkness in the Fold and darkness in Rew's house, for the lamp was extinguished.

The door was immediately dashed open. Lettie stood looking down upon him where he lay, with a great blotch across his eyes, and moaning, writhing like a snake that has been trampled on: *"Blinded, blinded—oh, my God! Blinded, blinded."*

Everything in the kitchen was smashed—tables, chairs, pictures—the poker lay in a corner, and the remains of the oil lamp lay on the floor.

"It was the lightning did it," said Lettie, with a gasp. "It was the lightning did it. He asked God to strike him blind, *and He did it."*

And she laughed a hideous laugh, while the thing on the floor rolled over and clutched the boot of the policeman.

Yes, Rew was blind, utterly, hopelessly; and as for years after he crawled about, a ravaged wreck of what he had been, the women pointed him out with a shudder as the man whom God had stricken blind.

A strangely altered man was he, and was the theme of many addresses by the missioners in the Fold for years after the children had ceased to dream of the Tree Tops.

Strangely altered, strangely meek and humbled when with Lettie at his side, he went through the Fold. And people marvelled as they watched the appealing dread on his face whenever it turned towards her, and said it must be remorse for the wrongs he had done

her.   But in the book of the Recording Angel
it is written that he went about in dread lest
she who with a common oil lamp had skimmed
the light from his eyes should some day as
suddenly and as righteously extinguish the
dark glare of his soul for ever.

CHAPTER IX

THE TREE TOPS

ONCE upon a time there were four little boys, who lived in a place called Tumblefold. It was a dark, dirty place, and everybody was poor. Indeed, some of the people would eat one meal, never knowing whence the next would come.

There were no gardens in Tumblefold. The only green thing was a single pot of musk in Yeubrey's window, and the children used to linger as they passed to look at its pretty little yellow flowers.

But in the summer the big children used to go out on holiday afternoons into the country, and come back with bunches of wildflowers, daisies, buttercups, dandelions, and sometimes bluebells or red and white may. The little ones, who were too young to be taken on these walks, crowded round in joy at sight of the beautiful flowers, and if, as a favour, they were allowed to smell the may, they were happy all night.

The big children, with such an air of mystery, often told them stories of green fields and pools of clear water; of cows and sheep and lambs, and of birds singing high up in the clouds or in the tops of trees (great big flowers which had only green leaves and no blossoms, and grew higher than the highest house in Tumblefold). The little ones listened with open mouths and wide eyes, and asked questions till the others grew tired of answering.

The little ones did not forget the stories. Under Yeubrey's window they stood in a row on summer nights, and stared far over the houses and roofs at a green, moving line of tree tops. They told wonderful dreams to each other, and wished till they almost cried for the time to come when they would be old enough and big enough to go with the others into the country.

These four little boys—and they were very little boys then; it was before Stubbs came—gathered every night to look at the tree tops. On summer nights, when the sunset filled the sky with red and golden glories, they watched the shifting fires fade and fade till the sky grew silvery pale. The last rays always lit up the tree tops, and when the dark clouds were drifting across the sky, and the Fold was growing chilly and gloomy, still in the distance they saw the trees, and the glory that lingered lovingly over them as if afraid to leave them.

At last they were gone from sight, and four little lads were alone with their dreams. But not for long. The stars came out, and the white wonder, the moon, sailed through the clouds—often hidden, but always coming out brighter and more beautiful. And as the moonlight fell on the dark stretch of roofs, and lit up the ground where the little ones stood, still far away they saw the mystery of mysteries—the tree tops. Remember, these little children had never seen a tree, nor a field of grass, even; so you may guess what a wonder the tree tops were.

These four little boys (they were in the infant school) used to wonder in their childish way about everything. Their wonder was always tinged by the superstitions of their elders. It was said to be wicked to point a finger at the moon. Why, no one knew. But not one of these boys ever dared lift a finger towards the moon, lest unthinkable terrors should befall him.

Wondering; always wondering. They wondered what Tumblefold would do if the moon and stars were taken away; they wondered how the moon held up so high in the sky without falling, and could never understand where the light came from. There was a legend which said that the stars were only little lamps which were lit in the sky every night and put out every morning by an invisible lamplighter named Tommy Tiffin. The children were told that if they stared at the sky for half an hour without blinking their eyelids they would see him at work. They tried very hard, but half an hour was a long time to keep from blinking. So they never saw Tommy Tiffin.

But the trees, far away as they were, were of the earth, earthy. Some day they might even be reached. Nobody knew quite where they lay; but there was no doubt in the children's minds that if they went straight down the Susbury Road they would see them, sooner or later.

There were many ideas as to their whereabouts. The favourite one was that the trees were in the garden of a king's palace, and the dream-glory of that palace and its garden was more to those lads than all the fairy tales in the world. They had a great wish to go out together to find it, but when they asked the big ones none of them knew or cared to join in the search, and when they asked their parents they were forbidden to go, and told that around the palace and its garden was a long line of a thousand big policemen, who caught all stray little boys and boiled them to death in a great big pot.

This was terrible at first, but these lads talked it over, till they did not see why they should not run between the policeman's legs, jump over the wall, and so get in. For a long time they talked about it, and at last agreed to go the very next holiday, in spite of their parents and the big ones, who said they would get lost, or run over by mad horses.

The holiday came at last. It was Pancake Day. All morning the first class in the infant school had been jingling quite loudly—

"Pancake Day's a merry, happy day,
    If you don't give us holiday we'll all run away."

All morning the school had been well-behaved and quiet, for fear the holiday might not be given. But at twelve o'clock the governess, with a smile, sent them home for the day, and they tumbled out of prison laughing and shouting.

The four little boys ran home, and in the afternoon met, each with something big under his waistcoat.

No one was about, but in fear and dread they crept along walls and under windows out into the street.

Down the street they trotted, till they came to the schools, now closed; then they paused.

"Which way shall us go?" asked Ryder.

"Down the Susbury Road," said Potter promptly.

"S'ppose we get lost?" said Yeubrey.

"Lost yer granny!" said Jones. "Come on!"

They went on and came to the suburbs. How they opened their eyes as they saw the fine houses, and the rail-encircled trees along the road!

The first tree they came to was a marvel! They walked round it, and stared at its trunk, its branches, and its leaves in boyish wonder, till a policeman came, and they ran off. It was the very first tree they had seen, and their astonishment was great.

"Do they walk about?" asked Jones.

"Shouldn't wonder if they did," said Potter, "else what are the railings for? To keep 'em from walking off." .

They trotted on, seriously debating what to do if they saw a big tree coming towards them.

It was a memorable day for those four boys, and they learned stranger things than ever they learned afterwards. Heedless as to where it led, they went along the road. There were blue skies overhead and not a speck of smoke. They looked through palisadings at the big houses, with green grass and flowers in front of them, and with such clean windows. The gate of one house was open and they walked carelessly up the long drive, smelling every flower they saw. A footman came out and ordered them off. They were very little, these lads, and as he saw their pale faces and worn clothes he was not harsh with them.

Potter wanted to argue the point. "Why can't we look round?" he asked, in remonstrance; "we ain't doin' any harm."

"This is a gentleman's house," said the footman, "and nobody can come in without leave."

"But why not?" asked Potter obstinately. "Anybody can come through our Fold!"

The footman did not see the point, and hurried them out.

This was a new development, and their spirits fell as they stood together in the road. But the sunshine, and the green grass brought new life to them, and they went on, laughing and singing. They reached the open country, saw great trees along the road and in the fields, heard the larks high in the air, and tried in vain to whistle them down.

"I wonder why it is?" said Jones. "Our pigeons always come down when I whistle 'em."

Just at this moment something white and shining fluttered past their faces.

"Hooray!" shouted Potter; "it's a butterfly. Let's catch him."

Hats were off in a second and away they rushed. The butterfly seemed to enjoy the chase and dodged wickedly across the road, up in the air, in and out among them, and at last skipped the bars of a closed gate, beyond which was a big house, all windows. There were several well-dressed children playing on the lawn. The four wanderers pressed their faces against the bars and looked in, breathless at the butterfly's audacity as it fluttered among the flowers.

"Look at him!" said Ryder excitedly. "He's smellin' the flowers. You watch if they don't turn him out."

"P'r'aps he belongs to 'em," suggested Jones.

"Ha, ha! I've got yer this time!" said a horrible voice, and they found themselves fast in the arms of a big policeman. Escape was impossible; so, conscious of having done no wrong, they just looked up at him and said nothing.

"What's yer names? Where do yer come from? What are yer after?" continued the policeman, whose eyes softened as he took in at a glance their helplessness.

Then altogether in a breathless gabble they told him what they were seeking, where they came from, and how they had been turned out of a garden, while the amused policeman stared and muttered to himself, "Poor kiddies!"

He walked along the road talking to them. No; he had never seen the palace, and the row of trees taller than all the houses in Wolverhampton. Didn't believe there was such a thing—somebody must ha' been coddin' 'em. Was it right that they should be turned out of that garden? Well, no, it wasn't hardly right. Poor little kiddies! He knew they didn't see many flowers in Tumblefold. But, all the same, if a gentleman had a garden, he kept it to himself. Why, even he, a great big policeman, couldn't go in without being asked. Why did the butterfly go in? Well-l-l, butterflies was different. Let 'em keep going to school, and learn their lessons, and never tell lies or steal things, and soon enough they'd know all about it.

"Time enough yet!" he muttered, "time enough yet! Poor little kiddies!"

Then he gave them a penny apiece, and told them to go straight on. They might find it— they might—but as soon as it began to grow dark they must come back.

Rich and happy, they went on. They saw no more houses, and only a few trees, while the fields were brown and bare. They were tired, and when they came to a low, green bank by the wayside they lay down, pulled out their small stock of food, and soon cleared it away, being hungry. Potter had a bottle of pop, which they passed round merrily. When it was empty they threw at the bottle from a distance, till they smashed it.

They lay down and talked over the day's adventures; but they were very tired, and the drowsy air, the humming of bees, the singing of birds, and the curious quietness, so different from the foul and noisy Fold, had a strange effect on them. One by one they went to sleep, and dreamed of the king's palace, and the garden, and the trees.

Shabby and dark, with pale faces turned upwards, they lay in the green grass. My lords and ladies went by in their chariots, and looked with sneering disdain on the sleepers. Others went by on foot, and turned aside a little. A clergyman, fat and old, just paused to look at them.

"Ah!" said he, with a sniff, "John must watch my garden to-night."

A girl came by, dressed in black, with a book in her hand. She was walking in the middle of the road, but crossed over and looked into their faces. Her eyes grew moist as she stood, and her lips moved; maybe in prayer. There was a shadow on her face before. It was darker when she went.

Suddenly one of them woke up, and shook

the others. It was growing dark, and for the moment they hardly knew where they were.

"We're lost," said Ryder, half crying; "and we haven't found the trees."

The others were in much the same state of mind, but remembering that the road was straight, they started to trudge back. It grew darker. There were no lamps on the road.

"Johnny Yeubrey," said Jones, suddenly; "are you afraid of ghosts?"

Ghosts! It was the one thought in all their minds. They looked fearfully round, and clutched one another tightly.

"Let's get in the middle of the road," said Potter; "they might be behind the hedges."

Holding fast together they went on, looking round in dread every minute. Dark shapes loomed monstrously in front, but turned out to be trees or hedges. Their fears grew. The wind in the trees, a flying bit of paper, or a cart in the distance set their hearts beating and their bodies trembling.

Ryder was looking up continually. Suddenly he shrieked out, "Look at the moon. *It's follerin' us.* It was overhead when we started back, and it's over our heads now."

Up went their eyes, and at the same time they started to run. As they ran the moon followed, the hedges seemed full of threatening figures, and as they looked back the most awful shapes seemed flying after them. And when at last, breathless, dusty, and sweating, they reached Tumblefold, they were in a queer state, *for the moon had followed them home!*

They had been missed, but nobody thought of looking after them, and their story was such an incoherent medley of gardens, policemen, ghosts, and moonshine, that they were packed off to bed—to go through again in their dreams, that night and for many nights after, the whole adventurous day.

The dreams always ended in finding the palace, and the garden, and the trees; but by day they never found them.

CHAPTER X

THE GHOST IN THE OLD MALT-HOUSE

ONE foggy, dismal morning, Jones came running out of the street with his coat buttoned over some very bulky object. "I've got something," he said excitedly.

Ryder chuckled. "Abreum, Abreum, what has thou got in thy bosom?" he inquired facetiously.

Jones declined to tell. "Guess," he said, and smiled.

We guessed, but wrongly, and gave it up. Then the coat was slowly unbuttoned, the treasure disclosed, and we formed a circle so that no outsider should see it. Ryder made a suggestion, which was at first rebuffed, then accepted and discussed with our usual volubility in a corner.

. . . . . .

Tumblefold was nothing if not superstitious. To its ignorant and degraded inhabitants the supernatural was real and natural. They lived in two worlds. That there were spirits watching by night and day their deeds, and preparing just punishment for iniquity, was to them a veritable truth. The knowledge of the risks they ran added a peculiar spice to their wicked doings, and the man or woman who in the course of a quarrel gave emphasis to a blood-curdling oath, did so with full belief in its terrible possibility.

Most of their superstitions were such as the common folk everywhere believe in. Others were more local and unintelligible.

It was held unlucky to see the first new moon of the year through a window, to let the new year arrive without having a spray of mistletoe in the house, to break a looking-glass, or to lay two knives across each other on a table. The breaking of a salt-cellar was a sure sign of death, so was the chirping of any vagrant cricket who chanced to remove to Tumblefold. It usually brought death, too, to the cricket, for hearths were flooded with boiling water, and even torn up to dislodge the thing of ill-omen.

For in Tumblefold death was a terror. In his case familiarity bred no contempt. In warnings and tokens of death all believed, for what house had not known them? Mysterious knocks and tappings, dislodging of furniture, the horrible feeling as of an invisible shape

brushing past as one went upstairs in the darkness; aye, and far-away but well-known voices
calling out in the bare silence of midnight the
name of the doomed one—every house had its
mysterious story to tell. Round the fire or the
table after every funeral each mourner had
some experience to recount; and to the
children, screwed up in corners, and listening
almost with suspended breath, there was no
barrier and no veil between the seen and the
unseen.

It was tacitly acknowledged by all that the
dead did not rest in their graves, but took a
morbid part and interest in the days and doings
of those left behind. This was not wholly
pleasant to look forward to, and if any woman
in the Fold were accosted and promised fulfil-
ment of her first wish, that wish would be that
she and hers might rest quietly in their graves
when the Lord thought fit to take them.

On the Lord's broad shoulders many bur-
dens were placed. It was so easy a thing to
do, to leave the gutters unswilled, the houses
and children dirty, and to stand at the doors
talking, when the children were down with
fever, and to wonder vaguely why the Lord
sent poor folk so much trouble. When the
doctor curtly suggested the free use of soap
and clean water, and the man with disin-
fectants came round, they were regarded by

the women as something worse than Atheists. The women believed in God, and His name was so useful to swear by. So with their sick, whether old or young, they seldom troubled greatly. With arms folded under dirty aprons they would say, "If the Lord thinks fit to take 'em, He will, an' it's no good our grumblin' one way or another."

They did not; the sick were left to a double fight with death and ignorance, and seldom came out best.

.   .   .   .   .

The night had closed on this particular day. The fog had lifted, but it was pitch dark. Even the solitary lamp seemed doubtful whether to face the blackness or not, and at last it went out.

At the same time an old Irish woman, who earned a few shillings weekly by sorting rags in a marine store, entered the Fold on her way home from work. Being Irish, she was of course superstitious to the core, and a devout Catholic in time of terror. She entered the narrow alley leading past the malt house into Irish Row. Knowing the ghost story she went on with eyes fixed in front of her, and never once looking at the huge old building she was passing. She came to the shutterless window; then by one of those weird impulses which force the spirit against its will to face its greatest dread, she slowly turned her head round, for a second only. In wildest terror she ran back, shrieking: "Holy Virgin, Mother o' God, forgive me for all I've done. I've been a bad un in my time, I know I have, but never, never again if I'm spared this once —only this once."

She flung herself into the first house she came to. At first she was so incoherent that her fright was not understood, and was charitably put down to drink. But at last she made herself clear. She had seen a ghost in the old malt-house. She averred it was no ghost, but Satan himself. She was walking through the alley, and came to that window. Why, she could not tell, but she looked towards it, and met, pressed against the rusty bars, not two inches from her own, a lurid mocking face, with eyes of fire.

Her shrieks had roused the Fold. The women stood in dozens at the entrance of the passage, shuddering and talking in whispers. The story was not doubted. All the unreasoning superstition with which their minds were filled held them helplessly there, and not one in the crowd dared move a step either forward or backward, though the ghost might come round the corner at any moment.

It was guessed at once. It was the ghost of the old man, the reputed miser, who had hung himself in that very place so many years ago. The buildings had been empty since then, and had never been opened even; so the old folk said. But the old man's ghost had haunted the place ever since. Not for years had he been seen, but footsteps had been heard traversing the long floors, and climbing the worn wooden steps, while knockings and noises had been heard times out of number from all parts of the building.

As they stood there a figure rushed on them out of the darkness.

"The ghost," shrieked several at once.

It was not the ghost, however, but a woman who had entered the Fold from the other end, and on passing the shutterless window had seen the same livid face pressed against the bars.

It was getting serious. Several women, whose homes lay beyond the passage, dared not venture, though they were hungry and tired, having just left work. What was to be done? A lad suggested fetching a policeman, and was promptly cuffed. Policemen were in bad odour in Tumblefold.

The men began to gather round, and were inclined to laugh at it.

"It's burglars," said one.

"Burglars! you owd fule," said his wife, witheringly; "did y' ever know burglars break in an empty house?"

The "owd fule" withdrew, and in spite of their fears the women laughed loudly.

Then another man, fashioned of sterner stuff, whom an hour in the Spotted Dog had made valiant, swore vehemently that there was no ghost. And for why? Because there was no such thing as ghosts. He believed not in ghosts, nor in God nor devil, he didn't; and he was going to have a look at this pertickler ghost and see what he had to say for himself, he was. His wife said he must not go, whereupon he said he would.

Just as he was starting there was another shriek. A woman averred she had seen a livid face peer round the corner. There was no light, so the man's face could not be seen, but his voice was shaky as he exclaimed with an air of contempt: "Shut up, yer fule! yer drunk! I'll give him ghost if I catch him. I'm a comin', Mister ghost."

He went. A few seconds after he had turned the corner there was a fearful yell. He came running back, trembling, with his teeth chattering and hair on end.

There was no doubt of it. He believed in ghosts now. He had been to the window. There was no face against the bars, but at the end of the long room he saw swaying from the ceiling the body of a man, with livid face and eyes of fire turned towards the window.

Several of the women began to cry.

"It's a Token," gasped one, "sent down from Hevven. There's sumthin' goin' to happen. P'r'aps the Fold's goin' ter be burnt wi' fire."

They had heard of Sodom and Gomorrah, and they knew that Tumblefold was no better than it should be. So the terrible possibility was silently accepted.

The ghost defier went in the Spotted Dog and stayed there.

Potter's father came down. He was sober, for once; but not through merit. It was the night before pay-day, and he was cleaned out. He heard the story, and doubted it.

"Go and see for yerself," said one of the women.

This was a direct challenge. He declined, but offered to go conditionally that they all followed behind. He went in front, and followed by the crowd, we five among them, entered the passage. He turned the corner. The women held each other tightly. A few more steps, and he was staring through the bars. The rest held back.

"It's all right," he said slowly. "He's there right enough."

Gradually curiosity overcame fear, and one by one they crept up till the crowd was packed together behind him, staring speechlessly through the long, dark room at a figure, with livid skeleton face and burning eyes, swaying, from a beam apparently, in the darkness.

Potter senior tried one of the bars. It was loose. He pulled it out, then another, and another. He placed his hand on the sill.

"Lord help us," said his wife, "what yer going t' do?"

"Ghost or no ghost, I'm going to face it."

Still the figure swayed there.

Heedless of entreaties he got through the window. There was a dull echo as his feet touched the floor, an echo that would not die. Amazed at his pluck they stood there in terror waiting for developments.

They heard his cautious steady footsteps and the long echo till he apparently reached the middle of the floor, and then stopped dead.

Then came a shout and a huge laugh.

"Why, bust me if it ain't a swede lantern. Haw-haw-haw."

He came out with the ghost in his hand, and laughed till he nearly choked. The crowd separated, swearing profusely, especially those whose suppers had been delayed.

The culprits were never found out. But we knew.

When Jones came with his prize that morning (purloined, I may mention, from a farmer's waggon in the street), our first impulse was to share it and eat it. For raw swede-turnips were a great luxury. Then came the suggestion to make a lantern.

We carefully cut out the inside and ate it. We left a socket for the candle, we artistically removed portions of the skin, leaving transparent eyes, nose, and mouth; then we foraged till we found half a candle.

The malt-house was an afterthought, and we never dreamed of the consequences. We had long ago found a secret entrance, and often played there in the day time. It took a great nerve to enter it at night, but we did so, strung the lantern to the beam, lit the candle, and fled.

In the distance it bore a striking likeness to a human face. The wind swayed it to and fro, but it never came to the window, and certainly never looked round the corner. Superstitious imaginations did all that.

CHAPTER XI

THE WOMAN WHO LAGGED BEHIND

"HUSH," she said, swaying her body monotonously in an effort to soothe the baby crying in her arms. *"Hush! You might almost know what's goin' to happen, the way you're cryin'."*

.　　.　　.　　.　　.

The great bell of the old Church was slowly, solemnly tolling.

Blinds were drawn, shutters were closed, and crowds of people were pouring into the Square from all corners. Mounted policemen were backing their horses into the crowd, and endeavouring to keep open the downhill way into Susbury Road.

There was an old mansion at one end of the square, and here every blind was down. Near this house the crowd was denser than else-where, and the doors never opened, but all eyes strained as if trying to penetrate the darkness of the vestibule. The red-coated Volunteers and the mounted Hussars all looked in the direction of this house with an expression of sombre importance as they hurried across the Square towards their headquarters, some streets away.

It was a warm summer afternoon, but a light and cooling breeze from the west was stealing across the square. There were but few clouds, and the blue seemed very far away. The sunlight fell on many faces; there were careless smiles on some, but others darkened even in the sunshine with an expression of waiting awe. And still as they talked in couples or excited groups all eyes turned towards the darkened house in curious expectation.

.   .   .   .   .

"Hello, Gregson, what's the matter here?" said a busy man to a friend, whom he recognised as he was irritably trying to jostle his way through the crowd.

"Why, don't you know?" said the other in astonishment, not unmixed with pleasure, as he began mentally to elaborate a long and copious account of the whole thing.

"Shouldn't have asked you if I had known," said the busy man, impatiently looking at his watch.

"Well," said the other, taken aback by the rebuff, "they are burying Johnny Roule."

"Who, the lawyer?" said the busy man, indifferently, "and are all these fools waiting to see him buried! Afternoon, I'm off."

"But wait a bit," said his friend, clutching his sleeve, unwilling to let slip such an opportunity of surprising even a busy man with unexpected news, "this isn't going to be a common funeral. He was Mayor two or three years ago, you know, and a big man at Christ Church——"

"Yes, yes, I know," impatiently.

"Well, wait a minute. He was major in the Volunteers, you know; so there's going to be a public military funeral, and the Mayor and all the Council are going to walk—in their robes, mind you—and the Volunteers and Staffordshire Hussars are going to march him down. It'll be the grandest funeral that's ever been seen in Wolverhampton," he ended, looking anxiously in the busy man's face, to see the effect of his words.

"Ah," said he, as the child's instinctive desire to see a show came back to him. "I think I'll wait. What time's the funeral?"

"Starts from his house there at two o'clock. Nearly that now. Time the Volunteers were here. The Mayor and the Councillors are waiting in the Town Hall. They are taking him to Tettenhall, you know, the family vault's there."

"Oh, aye! It's a two-mile march then—How old was he; what was the matter?"

"Not above forty—looked older, you know, but see what a life he led, women and booze all the time. Fine fellow he was, ten years ago. But a horse's constitution wouldn't stand his racket."

"No," said the busy man carelessly; " 'tisn't likely. I see that fellow Wilder's failed at last. I'm in for a hundred, are you in at all?"

"Only twenty. I never let him go too far. When's the meeting?"

And so they stood discoursing, forgetting the crowd and the darkened house over the way. For busy men have no time to speculate on deaths and funerals.

.　　.　　.　　.　　.

The Chief of Police cantered up on a spirited horse, and the policemen began to clear the people from the front of the house. A drum was heard in the distance, and the crowd, with the usual collective instinct, rushed to one end of the Square, and blocked the road along which the Volunteers were marching. Then, at a clatter of many hoofs, and the appearance of many waving plumes and glittering scabbards, the crowd scrambled backwards, and the Hussars cleared the way into the Square for the Volunteers marching just behind them.

With much manœuvring and ceremony, the Volunteers were ranged along two sides of the Square, and the throngs that crushed behind, and strained for a glimpse over their shoulders, saw many carriages rolling up, and great riding to and fro by the Hussars, as the procession was being formed.

But the woman who, with her babe in her arms, had crept up into the Square from Tumblefold—she stood back in the shadow of the buildings, away from the crowd. And perhaps she was better there, for the sunlight could only intensify, could never remove, the shadow on her face. But her eyes, like those of the others, were fixed on the door of that house.

And suddenly a low, hoarse murmur went through the Square, for the door opened, and a large coffin was borne out on the shoulders of six men, and laid on a gun-carriage waiting outside. They covered it with a Union Jack, and laid over him the sword and helmet he would never use again.

The Mayor, in his robes of office, preceded by his mace-bearer; the Town Clerk, in his wig and gown; the aldermen and councillors, in their black gowns, went to the front of the procession; the widow and other mourners, and many influential local gentlemen, in their carriages, lined up behind the riderless horse of the man in the coffin; the Hussars and Volunteers took up their positions, and the band began to play the Dead March in *Saul*.

Then slowly, solemnly, to the strains of the weird threnody whose passionate grief and heart-broken lamentation brought tears to the eyes of many women and some men, and a sudden foreboding gravity to the faces of the most careless and thoughtless, the long procession moved down the hill, and into Susbury Road; thence down, down again towards the village which lay at the bottom.

People lined each side of the road in hundreds, and a great crowd followed. The woman with her baby lagged behind, but never so far away that she could not see the flag-covered coffin on the wagon, and the beautiful black horse that hung down its head as if knowing the full import of it all.

. . . . .

"Man that is born of woman has but a short time to live, and is full of misery."

. . . . .

"Oh, he killed himself with pleasure, there's

no doubt of it," said one town councillor to another. "This is awfully slow, ain't it?"

" 'Tis that. Wish it was over. Yes, he knew how to enjoy himself, did Johnny. But he never objected to paying for it—most generous-hearted in his way—though he was a fool when he'd been on the racket for a week or two. D'ye remember the council meeting when he disappeared, and we found him in the ante-room with——?"

"Ha, ha; should think I do. Got well chaffed for it, didn't he? That was a splendid dinner he gave at the end of his mayoralty, though; knew how to do the thing in style, did Johnny."

"He did that. But this is slow. Why the devil don't the sun go down. The sweat's boiling off me."

The Mayor looked bored, though occasionally he smiled to himself as he saw the mace-bearer panting and sweating in front of him; for the mace-bearer was bulky and old. And they had yet a mile to go.

. . . . .

The widow's cheeks were stained with tears, but there was a look of strange relief in her eyes as she looked through the carriage window for the turning at the end of the road—

but she never looked at the coffin on the wagon.

.   .   .   .   .

"He cometh up, and is cut down, like a flower: he fleeth as it were a shadow, and never continueth in one stay."

.   .   .   .   .

"You've lost a good man in the Major," said a Liberal to a Conservative; "about the most popular man you had, and a good speaker— though he was a bit vulgar at times."

"He learned that before he left the Liberal party," retorted the other; "but, as you say, he was a good un, and we shall miss him."

"And his subscriptions," said the Liberal, with a knowing smile.

"Just so," said the Tory, laughing; "but he'd have romped in for the West Division next election."

.   .   .   .   .

A group of middle-class ladies stood on the lawn of an imposing villa, and gazed sadly at the procession as it went past.

"Ah," said one, "there goes a good man, if ever one lived. Scarcely ever knew him to miss attending church on Sundays, and he must have given away a small fortune in charity. I never had a rebuff from him when I asked for subscriptions, and at our last bazaar he headed the list with a cheque for a Hundred Pounds. What a dreadful shock it must be to his wife. Poor thing, how terribly ill she looks."

And there was a chorus of "Poor thing."

And a few minutes later they stared disdainfully at the ill-clad haggard woman who went past, with a baby in her arms.

.   .   .   .   .

"A clever lawyer was Johnny," said a magistrate to a racehorse owner, "and up to all the tricks of his profession. If he couldn't save a man's neck nobody else could. I've seen him—where there was a clear case for conviction, mind you—bully a whole Bench of Magistrates and force them, in defiance of evidence and law, to acquit his man. Made a lot of money, too, but he was a fool with it. *Do you know,*" and he whispered for some minutes, while the other smiled knowingly.

.   .   .   .   .

"Dry work, this," said the Clarionet to the Piccolo, during a rest from playing. "If old Johnny could see this show now he'd pay for drinks for the bloomin' battalion, 'e would."

"Aye, 'e waz a good sort," said the Piccolo,

"though I've bin told his servants give 'im an awful name for being close-fisted. I say, I've got a dead cert. for the Leger."

"Get out! What is it?"

. . . . .

"In the midst of life we are in death: of whom may we seek for succour, but of Thee, O Lord, who for our sins art justly displeased?"

. . . . .

"If ever there's a good God in Heaven, and a Devil in Hell, that man's in Hell this minnit," said a respectably-dressed woman, pointing at the coffin as it went by.

"What for?" said a bystander, turning round carelessly, to be met with a wild stare of hate and the convulsive utterance: "He ruined my daughter—the only one I had—oh, my God."

Those near closed round, seeing her sobbing; but the children went on with the procession, chattering volubly, and staring in wonder at the gay tunics of the Hussars and the Volunteers, and admiring the sheen of the swords and the helmet spikes. It was quite a field day for them.

. . . . .

The Woman's face grew white, and she trembled strangely as she saw the wagon turn down the little street that led to the church, for her home was in that street.

A year ago she was as pure and innocent as the roses in her father's garden.

And now—she lived in Tumblefold.

.   .   .   .   .

A group of working men stood looking on. Said one, vigorously—

"A dam good job he *is* dead! His sort ought to die. I remember him saying at a Tory meeting as fifteen bob a week ought to be enough to keep a workin' mon an' 's wife an' kids comfortable on? He ought to 'a' bin the fust to try it."

Said another, with a snigger, "He'd 'ave had a job to keep *all* 'is kids on fifteen bob a week."

[•]   [•]   •   •]   [•]

"I'll never forget this as long as ever I live," said many a woman in the crowd, "it's the grandest funeral as ever I've seen. He must ha' been a wonderful clever man, by all accounts."

[•]   [•]   [•]   •]   •

And so, after one of the most imposing demonstrations of Respect and Esteem for a departed citizen that had ever been seen in Wolverhampton, they buried the body of John Roule with full military honours in Tettenhall Churchyard, and the whole affair was, as the local paper said that night, "a magnificent token of the public's appreciation of the many elevating and noble qualities in the deceased gentleman's character, and will live long in the memory of all who were privileged to take part in it."

And the next day the world was working and toiling as industriously as ever, in spite of the great loss it had sustained. There are so many in the world who are universally respected and esteemed that we have learned to bear with resignation their removal to a higher and brighter sphere.

.   .   .   .   .

But when the last volley had been fired, and the merry quick march of the returning band had died away on the hill; when the vanished glint of the bayonets had left a strange darkness even in daylight, and the Hussars, and the Red Coats, and the noisy crowd had left the country road clear once more, the woman, who had lagged behind, entered the Churchyard, and wandered about till she found his grave.

And there, still clasping her babe—and his

—to her hunger-shrivelled breasts, she fell on her knees, and cried till long after the darkness had in pity closed around her.

Of his ambitions, hopes, ideas, and ideals she knew and had known nothing. Of his story she knew only too much, but he had told her that all men were the same, and she had believed him. And perhaps he was not so very far wrong.

And since he had deemed his splendid body not too great to mate with hers, she, not easily at first, but easily, eagerly afterwards, had given her body to him. But her soul went with it.

And though months ago he had deserted her, and only betokened that he remembered her by sending a few shillings weekly, since he had been to her the nearest and noblest man in the world, she wept on his grave.

And there was no one to comfort her.

For in her way—not a very great, nor exalted way, perhaps—perhaps only in a dog's way, although that may be as true and worthy as any other way—she had loved him.

CHAPTER XII

THE GREAT SNOW HOUSE

THERE was fun in Tumblefold. It was Christmas morning. A hard winter had set in, but trade was unusually good, and the wolf had so far been kept away. We five were in possession of good hobnailed boots, and played on our heels backwards through the frost-bound Fold.

On Christmas Eve it grew dull, then dark; and with the shades of night the snow began to fall. It was the first long snow, and we stood outside together, letting it fall thickly upon us, and chanting gleefully the childish jingle:

> "Snow, snow faster,
> Or else we'll tell y'r master."

Faster and faster it fell, as if in obedience to our injunctions. We revelled and rolled about in it as only boys can, till an avalanche in the shape of several mothers descended on us and lugged or drove us all indoors. But every now and again we opened the doors, and looked out into the night. Still snowing, and Tumblefold was deserted and silent, save for the hideous choruses that rolled up at times from the Spotted Dog.

Eleven o'clock came. We slipped down to the Spotted Dog, expecting the usual fights. But, no. They came rolling and cursing out into the blinding snow, already inches deep; and after sundry oaths of surprise, went homewards through the blinding snow. They could not fight in that.

Next morning, as with one accord, Tumblefold went to its doors, and saw a deep, untrodden bed of snow before it, which in some parts had drifted as high as the door latches and shutters.

The juveniles were out early, and soon a great snowball fight was raging, which at last resolved itself into five against the rest. Stubbs, as usual in fights, was in the way, and every snowball seemed to hit him. At last we bundled him inside his own door, and proceeded.

A bilious reveller put out his head to see the fun. Jones promptly potted him in the nape of the neck. After nearly standing on his head in a vain attempt to keep the snow from melting down his back, the bilious reveller strode out belligerently—to catch on his second shirt button a heap of snow from another reveller who enjoyed the fun.

This was the signal. Male and female alike, all were at the doors, but came out one by one, till the Fold was a laughing, crying, screaming mass of men, women, and children, pelting each other with huge lumps of snow, or rolling over and over in it, locked in each other's arms, utterly regardless of sex. Sometimes half-a-dozen together pitched headlong into a snowdrift. At last there were so many in the white war that an ordinary observer passing through would have distinguished only a kicking, half-buried mass of legs, arms, shirtsleeves, petticoats, dirty stockings, and flowing hair, choking or gasping for breath, yet screaming with maddest merriment.

The pace was too hot to last. An hour afterwards the juvenile tribe were again in possession, while with tingling fingers, streaming eyes and noses, and garments soaking with wet, the elders were roaring over the joke or blaspheming their senseless folly.

Even we came to a finish at last, and we five stood under our window stamping our feet, blowing our fingers, and marking the huge heaps into which the snow had been thrown.

Suddenly Potter exclaimed: "Let's make a great big snowball."

We jumped at the idea. Forgetting the cold, we picked up the biggest lump, and began rolling. At first we took it in turns, two rolling while the others warmed their hands. But soon the snowball had grown so heavy and big that it took all five to roll it along.

At last we stopped. We had come to a slight incline, and were half way up when it rolled back—on Stubbs, of course, who was in the middle. He was not really hurt, but was cold, and shrieked out "Mamma, mamma," as he always did when terrified.

"*Mammy, mammy,*" mimicked the roughs, who were watching us jealously.

We turned white and red. Then we fell on Stubbs, and bullied him. Why couldn't he say "Mother?" Mother was all right, though "our old woman" was better. Why didn't he drop his baby ways and say "Mother?" Who learned him to say "Mamma?"

"My papa did," wailed Stubbs.

That was worse. We stood staring at him, helpless and speechless. Potter exclaimed savagely:

"Look here, Freddy Stubbs, we ain't goin' to have any more o' this. All the kids are shoutin' after us 'cos you say 'Mammy.' You ain't any better off than us, and we don't want flash 'spectable ways at all. So you drop it. You hear, eh?"

"Y-yes," whispered Freddy, who was crying.

With injured feelings we turned to our snowball, and were just in time to prevent a handful of roughs rolling it away. Having rewarded them for their diligence, we started again to roll it up-hill. Jones was in the middle this time, and we grew quite hot.

"Push," yelled Jones, "it's coming back on me."

"We are pushin'," retorted Ryder, "you ain't pushin' a bloomin' ounce. Now, Freddy, stick to her."

"There's none of yer pushing 'cept me and Yeubrey," gasped Pottter, "why don't yer push?"

"Shut yer trap," exclaimed Jones, "push all of yer—quick, it's on my toe."

So shouting, pushing, and struggling, we rolled it to the top, and stood gasping round it, prouder than Wellington after Waterloo.

"Ain't it heavy," said Potter.

"Ain't it," said Jones. Then, reflectively, "I wonder how heavy it is?"

We all looked at Stubbs, who had had it on top of him. He saw his responsibility, and the shadow of deep thought fell on his face. Finally he said, slowly:

"Twenty-eight pounds one quarter—four quarters one hundredweight—twenty hundredweight one ton—it's over three tons?"

Potter and I whistled.

Ryder looked startled, then very uneasily began rubbing his back.

"I've sprained it," he said, explaining, "must have been the weight."

"Strike," said Jones, in awe. "Over three tons! What shall we do with it?"

That was a poser. We went in to dinner.

When we came out it was still there. It seemed to have grown. We stood round in silence.

"I say," said Potter in some alarm, "this won't do, you know. We shall have to shift it somewhere. If it rolls down it might kill somebody, or knock the end of Yeubrey's house in."

These were disasters we had not foreseen. Without more ado we decided to roll it into Jones' backyard. After a struggle, we managed it, and put it in a corner. We stood staring. Over three tons! It was a wonder.

Suddenly Potter cried, "I say. Let's make it into a snow house."

"Grand!" said Ryder, "and we'll sleep in it every night."

"I'll help," said Freddy, "I've got a chisel."

"Chisel?" said Potter, loftily, "what yer want a chisel for?"

"To cut the winders out," said Freddy, somewhat hurt.

Potter laughed loudly: "Oh, you soft, you don't have winders in a snow house."

"How shall we do it," said Jones, eager to begin; "shall we pull it to pieces and build the walls?"

"You shut up," said Potter, savagely: "I ought to know, didn't I? My uncle's in the Rifles."

Jones shut up. Potter eyed the monster critically and judiciously, and said: "It's in the corner, so we've got two walls out of four. We'll holler it out. That's it. We'll holler it out."

We agreed. Borrowing an old shovel from Jones' mother, Potter climbed on top, with assistance, and commenced "hollering out."

"Hi, what yer doing?" asked Ryder, in alarm. "Ain't yer goin' to have a roof?"

Potter turned round fiercely: "Look here, Ryder, are you hollerin out, or me?"

"You am, I reckon," said Ryder, sulkily.

"Well, you shut up. My uncle's in the Rifles, ain't he?"

That was unanswerable. Ryder retired, figuratively.

Nevertheless, Potter came off the roof and started hollowing out the middle.

We let him go at it for half an hour. Then we saw the joke of it.

"Look at him," whispered Ryder, "see how he's puffin'."

"Look at him," chuckled Jones, "he can hardly lift the bloomin' shovel."

A minute later he turned round, and caught us all laughing. He looked nasty.

"That's the way you do it, is it?" he inquired, dropping the shovel. "Just like yer. Stand by and see me do all the work. Here's the bloomin' shovel. Let somebody else holler out, I won't."

Ryder picked up the shovel, and went to work industriously.

But Potter had left the roof too thick, and part of it suddenly crowned in, and fell on the nape of Ryder's neck. He dropped the shovel, and jumped out violently.

"Who chucked that, I should like to know?"

We were bursting. Ryder went mad.

"It was you, Jones, yer bloomin' pig, it was. I see yer do it. Cock yer fisses up and I'll fight yer."

Jones was accepting, when we interfered, and cooled them down.

But Ryder was tired of hollowing out. So

we went at it in turn all afternoon till we finished the great snow house. It was four feet square and three feet high inside. We made two low seats of hard snow; these we covered with pieces of old bagging. The entrance was a low hole, through which we crawled. When all five were in, the house was full. We looked at each other in ecstacy.

"It's Grand," said Potter and Yeubrey.

"It's Wonderful," said Stubbs.

"It's perfectly spiffin," said Ryder and Jones.

All that week we were a sentinel corps, guarding Jones' back door, and letting in one by one all the juveniles in the Fold to look at the snow house. Sometimes, as a great favour, we let them creep inside.

We dreamt of it all night, and our first act every morning was to run round, and see if it still stood.

Every night for weeks, while the great frost lasted, we screwed ourselves inside for hours at a time, talking, singing, telling tales, and between whiles eating monkey nuts and smoking cigarettes. We indulged in the wildest visions of what we should do and be in the days to come, when schooltime was ended, and work days had commenced.

We had lights, too. We searched the ashheaps for fragments of candles, pilfered any odd ends we could find at home, and ran voluntary errands for odd halfpennies, with which we bought candles and monkey nuts.

But all things come to an end at last. One morning we ran outside, to find the rain coming down fast and pitilessly, tumbling over the spouts, and roaring down the gutters.

When we got to Jones' back door there was nothing left of the great snow house but a shapeless, dirty mass of mud, and snow, and water.

Our achievements were many and surprising before and after this. But nothing was ever like unto that Snow House. And to this day the children of another generation point out with awe and reverence the place whereon we built the Great Snow House.

CHAPTER XIII

THE TERRORS OF TUMBLEFOLD

POTTER began it, as usual. We were getting used to that. He led the way, and we loyally followed. He was the quickest and cleverest of the five, and though we were not backward, when it came to a test match in spelling or mental arithmetic we retired forthwith.

He appeared one night with that peculiar glow in his eyes which always betokened a surprise in store. After looking carefully round to see that no spies were about, he produced from his bosom a pamphlet with a red cover, on which was a blood-curdling picture of murder and sudden death. It was entitled: "Dick Deadeye, the Pride of the Prairies."

We closed together under the lamp, and Potter began in a low voice to read it out to us.

For several hours we listened breathlessly to the marvellous adventures of the Prairie Pride and his untameable mustang, Bonny

Brown Bess, who never knew saddle, and whom no other man than Dick Deadeye dared even stroke.—How, when a boy, his home was burnt by Red Indians, and his parents murdered and scalped, he only escaping; how he registered a vow of vengeance on all Red Devils, and thereafter waged a pitiless war against them; how he fought them in ambush and in the open; was captured once and tied to a tree as a target for knives; how Bonny Brown Bess rushed to the rescue, killed his guards, scattered the whole tribe, kicked out the brains of the chief Golly-go-gobber, then gnawed at the ropes till she had freed her master; how he and Bess faced alone whole herds of buffaloes, wild horses, and cowboys, coming off best every time and finally died together, flushed with glory and scalps.— Truly, it was a revelation to us.

Our world hitherto had been limited to Tumblefold and a few green lanes in Wolverhampton. Now, we had a stake in creation, and were eager to possess it. We had, it is true, been led to understand at school that Wolverhampton was not the world, and that if it were to disappear some night there would be other towns left. We knew that London was the capital of Great Britain, that Willenhall was famous for locks, Walsall for saddlery, Birmingham for German silver, and

Gornal for white sand. We were taught little beyond this. There was nothing in it at all to appeal to our feelings or our memories, or to suggest that the world was anything but a huge agglomeration of Tumblefolds and Susbury Roads.

But here was a story appealing to a boy's strongest weakness, his imagination, which revealed to us a world of which we had hitherto known nothing; a beautiful murderous world, with illimitable stretches of green, grassy plains, where at every step one might tread on a hidden snake or poisonous Indian. A world wherein, above all things, a man was free to think, and do as he chose, and might ride out daily under the warm sun and dark blue skies, with gun in hand and pistols in belt; taking even less thought for the morrow than did the old Bible fool. How could a man starve, or have need to work in a factory, when he had but to stand at his door, shoot a buffalo, and so provide his daily meals for a week?

The story was not finished that night, but the next. Then we began again, and went through it so many times that we wore it out by merely fingering the leaves.

Our natures changed; imperceptibly, but they changed. To us that story was true. A new element had entered into our lives. We had something to think about, to talk of by day and dream of by night, and a new world to look forward to.

We decided to make for the prairies on leaving school. Distance was no object; a mere minor consideration. We talked, always in corners, in quite a matter-of-fact way of the scalps we would take, the buffaloes we would slay, and the prisoners we would rescue on the prairies. Even Stubbs entered into it as eagerly as the others, and astonished us all by his bloodthirsty yearning for scalps.

A reckless act by Jones somewhat marred the picture. He had stolen his mother's clothes-line, and fashioned it into a lasso. With Stubbs for his buffalo, he proceeded to show us how he would do it on the prairies. The lasso, however, missed the buffalo and went through a window, which cost Jones sixpence, to say nothing of a hiding with the lasso.

We had gone too far, however, to retreat or think of retreating. Every penny we could get bought a new specimen of our favourite class of literature, till we carried them hidden about us by the dozen. Each was devoured breathlessly and shared round.

Even now, after many years, I question if they ever did any one of us the least amount of harm. They made amends for the monotonous dullness of school lessons; they lit

with imaginative incident a bare palling
existence, and they prepared the way for an
appreciation of something better. That something better was never shown to us at school.
Of the masters in English literature or fiction,
even, we knew nothing till we were old enough
to become borrowers from the free library.
Then, instinctively, we made our way from
Marryat to Dickens.

In that first craze, which lasted for months,
we tasted life and breathed bravery in every
page.

Each of us was the Midshipmite Jack, the
Buccaneer Bill, and the fearless footpad of
the story. We were the drummer-boys who
came back with Napoleon from Moscow; we
helped to win Waterloo; we alternately fought
with and as pirates on the Spanish Main; we
were with Nelson when he fell; we came home
laden with the spoils of the great Armada;
we were outlaws with Robin Hood in Sher-
wood Forest; we joined with Richard the
Lion-hearted in the Crusades; and we sailed
with Columbus till he discovered America and
the prairies—the free, illimitable prairies, to
say nothing of snakes and Injuns.

Then Ryder brought a story of a different
kind, dealing with the surprising life and adventures of Daredevil Dick, the honest high-
wayman, who robbed the rich and fed the poor,

till an undiscriminating public gathered to see him hung at Tyburn.

This story appealed strongly to us and our sentiments. The prairies were not in it. This was an English story, and might even have had its counterpart in Wolverhampton. We admired Daredevil Dick, and sincerely lamented his untimely end. He had in our estimation lived a noble and virtuous life. It could be no crime to rob the rich and give to the poor; even Stubbs agreed with that. Boys though we were, we had already found out that too many rich people live by robbing the poor.

So when Ryder proposed forming a secret society of Daredevil Highwaymen, we hailed it with joy; then, as usual, fell to talking it over.

Visions of unlimited booty brought joy to our eyes. We saw ourselves, after a few years of valorous effort, returning to Tumblefold in our carriages, amid the enthusiastic cheers of the whole townspeople. We would marry our present sweethearts, and provide them with gold rings and brooches galore; we would pull down the Fold, with its rookeries and dens, and build each dweller a neat little cottage; we would build five villas in the middle, with stables and coachhouses complete; in these we five would live and flourish, and take our wives and the old folks a drive into the country every morning of every day in the week.

"But," suggested Stubbs, hesitatingly, "s'pose we gets hung, like Daredevil Dick did?"

Potter promptly pulled his nose, with an expressive "yah!"

"Just serves you right, Freddy," was the verdict. All the same we were somewhat disturbed in mind. It was just possible that we might be as much misunderstood as was Daredevil Dick. So we decided to begin in a small way.

We had, we considered, the right of way through Tumblefold, at least; and decided to levy toll on all rich strangers who passed through after dark.

For weapons we had two penny toy pistols, and two rusty bayonets, the property of Ryder, who had begged them from a brother employed in a marine store.

"They want polishing a bit," he said, apologetically, as he produced them.

They *did*. We took turns at polishing for a whole week, and they still needed polishing. So we took them as they were.

We apportioned the weapons, but could not trust Freddy with one. His duty was to strike an attitude, and shout, "Stand and deliver—r—r."

"But I say," said Jones, "what about names? We must have names, you know."

"You shut yer face," said Potter, loftily; "I'll settle that. I tell you what, we'll be the Terrors of Tumblefold. I'll be Dick Dead-eye, Ryder will be Jonathan Wild, Yeubrey and Jones—why, you'll be Robin Hood and Little John, of course. Then there's Freddy Stubbs, you'll be—you'll be—"

He looked at Stubbs, half reproachfully.

"You ain't very big, ye know," he said.

"N—no," said Freddy, rather abashed.

"And you're easily frightened."

"Ye—yes," humbly.

"So if we call you the Little Terror you'll try and deserve it?"

Freddy promised, glad to get off so lightly.

"There's another thing," said Potter, gravely; "we must take an oath."

"Do it on the Bible, of course," said Jones.

"Won't do," said Potter, "must be done in blood. One of us must be stuck in the arm, we must dip our fingers in his blood, cross swords and pistols on it, and take our dyin', solemn oath never to split. Who's it goin' to be? Come on, fingers in the pie."

Fingers in the pie it was, round Ryder's cap. Potter began solemnly: "Awkum, baw-kum, booney kawkum."

It was a terrible time. I came out first, and

was greatly relieved. Stubbs came out next, and then Jones. It lay between Potter and Ryder. Potter was quite calm. Ryder was very white.

"Akerbo, akerbo, twenty-one, it's you," said Potter to Ryder; "turn yer sleeve up. Jones 'll stick yer with his knife."

Ryder refused point blank.

Said he: "It's a plant. He's done it a-purpose. I always get in for it when he fingers."

Potter retaliated, and the row became so serious that all thoughts of blood-letting had to go. So we took a very mild oath over crossed bayonets to remain true, and tight, and not to split.

A few nights later one of the "rough lot" was whistling his way down a dark, lonely passage of the Fold when suddenly, as he averred afterwards, about fifty men with masks on sprang on him out of the darkness. They fired pistols at him, struck at him with swords, and tried to rob him, they did. But he was too quick for 'em, he was.

As a matter of fact he fled howling with fright as soon as he heard our war-whoops. Still, our first venture was a success, and we chuckled accordingly, although we had bagged no booty. The terror had begun.

The next comer was a big man, but we went

for him. Our war-whoops, however, were somewhat mixed, and the pistols would not fire. They were evidently made in Germany. To our surprise the man struck out fiercely with his fists and feet, and walked away swearing. We rubbed our bruised bodies in our hidden lair, and ruefully compared injuries.

"This'll never do," said Potter, gloomily. "This is the second go we've had, and we've caught nothin'."

"Only a good hidin'," said Little John, rubbing his head.

However, we hoped for the best, and laid wait.

"Hush-h-h!" said Jonathan Wild, although no one had moved, "there's somebody comin'. Get ready. Now don't forget yer words this time. Gi'e me a cap, quick. Get ready. Now!"

We jumped out. It was a grand success. The pistols went off, the bayonets flashed, and the unhappy man fell on his knees at the fearful shouts:

"Yer money or yer life!"

"Put yer hands up!"

"Move another inch, an' yer a dead man!"

"Stand, or I fi-er-r-r!"

Alternately cursing and protesting, the unfortunate man emptied his pockets of twopence-halfpenny, which he protested was all he had. We hesitated as to letting him off at that. It seemed derogatory to the profession —almost like blacklegging it.

"Do let me go, gen'l'men, do!" he pleaded, "an' I'll put you on a real good thing." With an air of mystery he told us, "In about ten minutes there's a man will come down here with a big coat on, half drunk. He's just come home from Callyforneyer gold diggin's, an' he's got thousands of pounds all in gold in his belt. It's true. I've seen it. You get that belt."

We let him go, which he did in a hurry.

Here was an adventure. We should be rich the first night! And as we lay in our lair we began to divide it amongst ourselves. Half an hour went by, but no digger appeared.

"It's a sell," said Ryder, savagely; "I knowed it was."

"What's a sell?" retorted Potter. "Why, he's comin'. Get ready; quick. Who's got my bay'nit?"

It was true. There was the man, the drunken walk, and the long overcoat.

We pulled ourselves together. This was a crisis in history.

"Mind, now," said Potter. "The belt!"

Out we jumped, altogether, with the usual shots and whoops—to find ourselves caught in the biggest pair of arms ever made, while a terrible voice shouted, "Come on, my little pyrits; the police station's your road."

There were only four of us. Stubbs had disappeared. It was a shocking experience. The policeman bullied, threatened and tried to thrash us; but failed, fearing the loss of some of us. So he took us home one by one, explained the case to our astonished parents and advised them "to keep them penny dreadfuls out of our road." Then he left us.

Figuratively, we had beans for supper. Sufficient for that night was the supper thereof. Yet we left a little for Stubbs when we took him to school next morning.

"You're a mean deserter," said Potter, severely, "and you ought to be shot."

And Stubbs, the inoffensive, timid Freddy, laughed in his face.

CHAPTER XIV

OUR PANORAMA

FOR several weeks the walls of Wolver-hampton had been covered with posters illustrating the wonders of the world. Among them were a number of pictures, large as life, of the chief events in the Egyptian war, then just ended.

Every morning we stopped, staring in admiration at two vivid representations of the cavalry charge at Kassassin and the battle of Tel-el-Kebir. We arrived, as a consequence, late at school, and received the usual caning. But no sooner were we out than we trotted to the nearest posting-station.

It was Sandie's Diorama and Trip Round the World. The journey occupying just three hours, with intervals for music and refreshments. All for the sum of sixpence, children under twelve half-price, and babies in arms not admitted.

We went. We saved up our pennies for a fortnight, then presented ourselves in a body. That was a memorable night. The pantomime was not to be compared with it, while Punch and Judy thereafter were counted as frauds.

We saw the pictures of the world and its wonders, from Charing Cross to New York harbour; we laughed at the patter of the man with the long stick, who pointed out the pictures, we applauded the wonderful talking dolls, and held on to our seats as we saw the battle pictures with realistic effects, real guns, real powder and fire.

We were so enthralled that when it was all over we sat staring at the "Good-night" scene, in the vain hope that it would pass, and reveal something else. But no! We sat till the gas went out, then we went out in a hurry.

We could not go again, having spent all our money. But for several nights we loitered round the back of the hall waiting patiently, and it always came; the boom of cannons, the roar of artillery, and bursting of shells at the great battles of Kassassin and Tel-el-Kebir. We were satisfied even with that; we could imagine the rest, although we missed the red fire.

We talked about it for weeks after. Then came an inspiration, not to one, but to all of us. Why not make a panorama of our own, exhibit it with realistic effects, and charge for admission? There was money in it, and it would be an act of philanthropy, too. The children of Tumblefold had never seen a panorama, and it would be a wonder and delight to them. Certainly, it would not be on so lavish a scale as that we had seen, and the realistic effects would be less tremendous, but what they had not seen they could not possibly miss.

"It's as easy ·as can be," said Potter, excitedly. "It needn't cost above sixpence. We'll beg a cigar box, put two rollers in it, then we'll buy a penny book of pictures and a candle behind it, it'll be a first-rater."

"I've got a twopenny box of paints," chimed in Freddy, "I'll paint the pictures."

"Good old Freddy," said Potter.

"I say, what about the guns?" said Ryder.

This was an important point. We talked it over, and decided to make the panorama, and put it on the top of a tall table in Jones' back kitchen. To keep the mystery complete and heighten the interest we would improvise a curtain, so that Potter alone would be visible, while we remained behind and worked the panorama and the fireworks. These latter were to be reserved for the battle pictures, and consisted of one penny box of percussion caps for the rifle shots, a pennyworth of red light for the fire, and a pennyworth of powder for the final explosion in the fall of Sebastopol.

The next few nights the voices under our window were silent. We were busy in Jones' back kitchen making the curtain, and painting pictures in colour combinations weirdly startling and effective; Potter inventing the patter for the pictures while we were painting away. It would be a bigger affair than we had expected. The views were quite six inches wide and four inches high.

We were at a loss for our battle pictures. The battle of Sebastopol was hard to get. So we had to make shift with two pictures from the last number of *Jolly Boys,* representing a pirate fight at sea and a battle between cowboys and Red Indians. These were coloured to do duty respectively for the Battle of Trafalgar and the Death of Nelson, and the fall of Sebastopol.

Having finished it to our satisfaction, we were fixing a night for a rehearsal when Jones discovered that the rollers had been forgotten. At first there was consternation, then the ever ready Potter went out and borrowed two skewers from the nearest butcher, while we heated the thin end of the poker and burned the necessary holes in the cigar-box. To make certain, we fixed the panorama, consisting of thirty views, on the rollers, and after several tries managed to make it work, with a certain unsteady wobble which had to be given up in despair.

Next night we had a rehearsal. The window was closed up, the panorama was mounted on a tall box on the table, and a candle lit behind it.

Jones went behind the curtain and began turning the rollers. We stood in front criticising, while Potter gave selections from his patter.

There were one or two slight hitches. Jones, who was standing on a chair which had seen better days, suddenly disappeared from view with a terrific bump. We grinned aloud till a sudden burst of smoke showed that the candle had fallen over and was burning the cigar-box. This was alarming but was soon put right, while Jones stood rubbing his head and abusing us for laughing at him—in his own back kitchen, too!

We went on again; this time without a fault, till Potter, who was standing on two bricks to lift him above the audience, slipped, and poked his stick through the picture on view.

"Go it!" yelled Jones, "break the blooming show up before we've begun."

"How could I help it?" snapped Potter. "You balance yerself on two bricks for half-an-hour and see what you'll do."

"What about me!" inquired Jones, sarcastically; "this chair's only got three legs and one o' them's broke."

We patched the picture up and continued. To our eyes the illuminating power of that one candle was quite equal to limelight. We came to the two battle pictures. They were gory and glorious, but—but—but——

"I say," said Ryder, hungrily, "let's have just a *little* bit of fireworks. We shall have plenty left."

He had voiced the common yearning. We went behind, struck half-a-dozen caps, and lit a little red light, while we peered round the corner to see how it worked. Our eyes beamed.

"It's a real battle picture now," said Ryder; "it's mag—mag—magnisifent."

So said all, except Potter, who was too well pleased to correct Ryder's little mistake.

We made the final arrangements. Potter would keep order and act as guide; Jones would show the pictures; Freddy was permitted to light the red fire for the battle pictures; and Ryder and I had the responsible office of hitting the caps with a hammer, pounding an old tray, and lighting the gunpowder.

The price of admission was an important question, pocket-money being scarce in Tumblefold. So we decided to charge a farthing a head, or its equivalent in rags and bones. Then we parted.

We left the panorama and curtains fixed, and Jones locked the door and took the key to bed with him. Thereby nearly came disaster. Jones senior went to work at six next morning as usual. He went to the back kitchen for his morning wash, and found it locked up and the key missing. So he promptly pulled the door down. Jones junior heard it, and fell downstairs just in time to save our treasure from the fire, for his father was very angry.

Next night we were all five at the back door, keeping a mutinous crowd at bay. We had carefully advertised it all the week, and the youngsters had grown quite anxious to see the panorama with real guns and thunder. So here they were in a giggling, noisy heap, just three times as many as the kitchen would hold.

We decided on the spot to run the show for a week, and loudly announced it. But no; they all wanted to see the first performance, and pushed and jostled and finally charged the five of us through the door, and packed the room. Potter and Jones rushed to the show, and the others went round collecting the fees. Farthings were few, but rags and bones were many, and so generously had they been brought that soon we had a big heap piled in a corner.

We disappeared behind the curtain; Potter remaining in front, wand in hand. His wand this time was a penny walking cane. Then the fun began. The children were laughing and yelling, and trying to find out how the show was being worked; but as the only light was the candle behind the pictures their curiosity was not satisfied, and of course grew greater.

Potter, whose abilities were held in great respect, shouted imperiously, "Silence!" Then a little savagely to those nearest him, "*Will* yer keep back? Do yer want to push me off these bricks?"

He had four this time, but his perch was far from safe. Rising to the occasion, he remarked over the curtain to Jones, "Get in your place." We were under the table, waiting the signal for fireworks. Jones got in his place. His head was just visible, and there was a yell: "It's old Jones. I can tell 'im by 'is 'air. Look at it. Carrots!"

Jones grew angry. His hair was not red, though it was a little rusty. But the wily Potter began.

"Ladies and—and gentlemen—er—Ladies and gentlemen. The performance is now about to begin. As you—er—know—we are about to take you—this evening—on a tower round the world, to finish up with the Battle of Sebastopol, an' if you noisy lot at the back ain't goin' to shut up take yer rags back an' go out—with real cannons and fire." ,

Jones began busily turning the rollers, amid approving cries from the audience.

"Don't 'e do it splendid?"

"Ain't it a treat?"

"Oh-h-h-h!!!"

Potter proceeded. "The first picture you see shows us Wolverhampton Station an' our train just startin' out. There's only the engine, because our panorama isn't like a real big un, you know, but if it was you'd see the station, and the carriages, and—and——"

"Shine yer bootser?" suggested one of the audience.

"And the shoeblacks," said Potter, affably. "The next picture shows you the ship we goes on, called the *Great Eastern*. It is a big ship, ever so much bigger than the boats on the canal. All the blue you see below it is the sea and the waves; all the blue above it is the sky.

"From there we take you to—to—— This is a 'Bull fight in Spain.' This man you see gets killed in the story, only they didn't put it in the picture. Then we go to—no, we don't, this is 'Sullivan,' the champion fighter. Then we go to the 'Falls of Niagara,' which is also in America—and the 'House that Jack Built' just comin'—don't turn it so bloomin' fast, Jones—this is 'Red Riding Hood'——"

"No, it ain't, it's yeller," shouted the audience.

"Yes, it is yeller," agreed the showman, "you see we used all our red paints in the battle pictures, and we had to paint her yeller, but it looks just as good."

"No, it don't," shouted a dissatisfied one at the back, "gie me my money back."

"I should just think you would," said Potter, sarcastically, "after you've seen half the show. We should be dummies. What are yer turnin' at?" to Jones, "can't ye see I've stopped talking?"

But Jones was grinding away, and Potter had to jump on. "This is 'Buff'lo Bill's Last Ride'—— No, it isn't, it's another ship. Oh, yes, so it is, this is the good ship—er—I just forget what, anyhow—this is it—'Buff'lo Bill's Last Ride' after the battle of—— What d' yer think yer doin', yer big-headed, fat-headed loonies." (This was over the curtain to Ryder and me. The signal for fireworks was "battle," and of course we began hammerin' the caps.) "This ain't the battle. There's no fireworks in this!"

We ceased firing, and got ready again. Potter and Jones went on. But the audience had heard us behind the curtain, and grew feverishly eager to look behind, and see how it was being worked. Potter grew desperate, and relapsed into the vernacular as they pressed on him.

"This is 'Gen'ral Gordon in the Desert'—come out o' that, want to push the bloomin' thing over? I'll hit yer on top o' the yed if y' don't drop it, Billy Turner—Gen'ral Gordon, I say, ridin' 'cross the desert to—to—Kartum, I think it was, but—will yer stop it before I hit yer with one o' these bricks. You want the battle and the guns? Do yer? Well, y' won't 'ave 'em till they come and that won't be till last. Now, are yer satisfied? An' y' won't 'ave 'em at all if yer don't leave off pushin'. This is 'Robinson Crusoe, and 'is man Friday.' This is the desert island, behind 'em, these up the top corners are trees, and this—will yer keep off these bricks? The battle pictures are comin' on, an' you'll see the guns an' the fire—they can't come on before their turns, can they? Why' it's here, now then, Battle!" over to us. "Ah, would yer?" knocking several back with his stick, "this, ladies and gentlemen, is 'The Death of Nelson an' the Battle of Trafflegar.'"

"Oh—h—h——!!!"

It was glorious. The guns went off, the tray

was banged, and the red light lit the room. Then, alas, for childish curiosity.

Just as the Battle of Sebastopol came on there was a mad rush to look behind the curtain. Potter was knocked from his bricks on to the curtain, which broke down, revealing Yeubrey kneeling on the floor and hitting caps with a hammer, Ryder banging the tray on his knee, and Stubbs lighting the red fire with a match.

Before we knew quite what had happened the crowd at the back had rushed the others on top of us, and the table, show, and Jones collapsed. The show caught fire and the candle fell on the gunpowder, which lay ready for the finish-up. There was a shock which shook the house and when the seniors opened the door they found a shrieking mass of children trying to get out, the table in flames at the other end, and the unfortunate Panorama Company fighting promiscuously with the biggest lads.

·   ·   ·   ·   ·

An hour later we stood in Jones' backyard moodily taking stock. We went through the rag and bone heap first and found we had been swindled. A lot of the children had simply wrapped a piece of rag round a fragment of brick and so gained admission.

We worked it out as follows:

Expenditure		Receipts	
By pictures	3d.	7 at ¼d. .... 1¾d.	
" Paints	1d.	Sale of Bones, etc. 2d.	
" Red Light	1d.		
" Caps	1d.	Total .... 3¾d.	
" Powder	2d.	Loss .... 6¾d.	
" At least 10 who must have got in for nothing	2½d.		
Total	10½d.	Total ...... 10½d.	

Besides this, our whole stock-in-trade was destroyed. It was a facer. Profits and properties—all were gone. So the company was dissolved by mutual consent, and the Great Panorama was withdrawn after a brief but brilliant run of one night.

CHAPTER XV

THE MURDER IN IRISH ROW

REALLY, it was not a Row at all. Towards the end of Tumblefold, where the hill sloped down to a stretch of low buildings which dwarfed the vicinity even more when contrasted with the tall old buildings which hung round the main square, was a narrow gully, just wide enough for one person to pass through. On one side was the wall of Claydabber's house, on the other was a gable of the old malt-house. This gully apparently ended in a pudding-bag arrangement of slum shanties. But as you turned the corner of the malt-house you found yourself in another gully, no wider than the other, in which four low cottages faced the desolate walls and window-bars, rusty with age, of the haunted malt-house. The malt-house was high and the cottages were low, wherefore it was always dark within them. This gully apparently ended in a brick wall, but two gullies led from its end; one leading through yet more passages into a street which skirted the lower end of the Fold, and the other leading into the back yard of the Spotted Dog—a huge area which might have held five hundred men easily. It had done so in the days of cock-fighting and prize-fighting.

This narrow passage, which was called Irish Row because the dwellers in those four cottages were of Irish extraction, was conveniently near to the Spotted Dog; for on Saturday nights, when work was good, there were always some little differences which could only be settled in a place sufficiently quiet and secluded. And policemen never came that way on Saturday nights. A fight in Irish Row was always re-freshingly vigorous, for it was so narrow that if a combatant struck at his man and missed him, he was sure to hit either a brick or a win-dow shutter. And the knowledge of the risk added considerably to the interest and excite-ment of the onlookers, especially when the fighters were strangers and did not know.

There was not much intercourse between the dwellers in Irish Row and those in Tum-blefold. There were several antipathies which explained all.

One was racial. The slow, stolid brains of the Staffordshire folk were ever suspicious of the volatile, passionate, and inexplicable natures of the Irish, who pulsed through a dozen differing moods while they were trying to follow them through one.

Another was sectarian. The Tumblefolders, when it came to a matter of sending for a clergyman to pray at a deathbed, relied on the Church of England to carry them through. The Irish were Roman Catholics, and were religiously hated—on Sundays. On weekdays faith grew tolerantly elastic, and they fraternized. But on any day the sight of two veiled nuns or a clean-shaven priest passing towards Irish Row provoked their sensitive foes, and the children ran behind in dozens, making derisive crosses in the air with their fingers, and crying:

"Catholic, Catholic, quack, quack, quack,
Go to the devil and never come back."

—while their elders stood on doorsteps and looked on approvingly at the staunch young defenders of their faith—who never went nearer than a dozen yards of the entrance to Irish Row, where the outraged Catholics were waiting in furious wrath.

And so, although the Irish residents were orderly and, on the whole, as law-abiding as their neighbours, they were never in good odour with them. And after what befell in Irish Row one long past Easter night, they were as pariahs and outcasts for ever.

Long books have been written about many a love story not nearly so pretty as theirs. But they were only common folk, and Irish at that.

Kathleen Crone was a typical Irish girl, queenly in form and figure, with beautiful dark-brown hair, and eyes of shadowed hazel, that could always express in fascinating eloquence her thoughts and emotions when the limited powers of oral expression, gained in a few years schooling, failed her.

On week-days she was only a rag-picker in a marine store; and even then, if you but looked for the soul in her eyes you forgot the degrading environment. A lily is never less pure for the putrescence in the soil it grows in.

When Jerry M'Carthy, in a glow of patriotic fervour, inspired by a combination of beer, judiciously administered, and the rapid eloquence of a calculating drill sergeant, "went and 'listed for a soldier," Kathleen was only a girl. She was a woman when he came home to Irish Row on his first furlough; and time had changed them both, and in the process had greatly improved them.

Jerry had been a hulking lout of a lad, shiftless and easy-going, good-natured and good-tempered, who handed over a fair share of his wage (he was a bricklayer's labourer) to his mother on Saturday afternoons, and spent the remainder convivially in the next few hours.

When he came back from "sojerin'," erect, ruddy, and strong, his mother said he was a Beautiful Boy, and even the Tumblefolders agreed with her.

For a fortnight he was a hero, albeit he had never been out of barracks. He treated all his old playmates and workmates, bought a new suit for his father, a new gown for his mother, and a brooch of "solid gowd" for Kathleen Crone. The two had been reared together; were good friends until he went away, and now, as their kinsfolk saw with approval, they spent much time together.

When Jerry's savings were spent, public interest in the returned traveller went quietly down, and Jerry and Kathleen sat in the midst of Irish Row night after night. Jerry told his history over and over again, while Kathleen looked with wide eyes in his handsome face. There seemed to be an understanding between the two. The others, having passed their time of understandings, passed round the quart jug till it was empty and Jerry paused in his story to order its replenishing.

And so the days went round till the last night came. The last night at home, maybe for years, maybe for ever; for Jerry was booked for six years in India and his old folk were getting very old and weak.

That night there was a farewell gathering in M'Carthy's. All the residents in Irish Row were there, including Mary Mulloy, a pale but pretty girl, whose sombre black eyes seemed always gazing through space in an endeavour to find Denis Regan, the sweetheart of her schooldays, who had gone to America years before to make a fortune for himself and Mary. And as she sat on the fender with the rotund form of her old mother keeping the dim light of the oil lamp from her face, she rested her elbows on her knees and her chin in her hands and wondered, as she watched Jerry and Kathleen sitting quietly together, if the home-coming of her Denis would be as solemn as this home-leaving of Jerry M'Carthy.

For the passionate love of home and kindred, which is aye at the heart of every true Irish-man, was strong within him, and the wild, weird mood of depression which dogs their effervescent merriment and makes life a series of intermittent falls from heaven to hell for this vivacious, passionate race, had fallen upon

him. And while the jug and the jest were cir-
culating merrily round the room, his eyes were
moodily staring earthwards, as the girl on his
knee whispered from time to time: "Don't go
back, Jerry; whatever will I do if you go and
leave me again? For six years, too. Why, I'll
be an old woman by then, and what will Jerry
M'Carthy be doin' to marry an old woman?"

And Jerry replied, without looking at her
face: "It's no good, Kathie! I'll have to go.
For if I didn't go back I'd be jailed as a deserter, and have to serve me time into the
bargain. No, I'll have to go."

And then he swore; still without looking at
her. But at last she placed her arm round his
neck, laid her head on his shoulder, and
whispered once again, "You won't go, will
you, Jerry?"

Athrill with the nearness of her body, he
looked at her beautiful face, marked the poise
of her splendid young figure, and the slightly
flurried heaving of the breast so near to his
own. And then he thought of six years in
India, while that sweet, bonnie creature—his,
and his only—was losing the glow and grace
of youth on the gloomy journey agewards.

His eyes stared widely in front of him; hers
watched his closely, anxiously. By nature
irresolute, hesitating, he was one of those men
who once in their lives can nerve themselves,

with the aid of sudden, surging passion, to some desperate resolve and carry it through, while paralysed reflection waits the result.

Jerry did this twice in his life. This was the first time. She felt a tremor in his arms as a strange look came into his eyes. Then he hurriedly released her, walked across the kitchen, unnoticed by all save Mary Mulloy. The others were growing noisily merry. He passed into the little room beyond. They heard him stumbling in the darkness, then at the click of metal against a stone, and then against something soft, yet hard, followed by a low cry, the girls sprang up and followed him. He turned, his face distorted by a look of pain and sardonic pleasure. His left hand was behind him, but there was blood on the floor and on a little axe in his right hand. There was something else on the floor. Jerry had rendered himself incapable of any further service in Her Majesty's army by cutting off one of his fingers. With due regard to economy, and the contingencies of civilian life, he had selected the little finger of his left hand.

The two girls saw, but did not faint. They bound up his hand, and hurried him through the back door to the nearest doctor, who looked queerly from one to the other, but said nothing as he finished dressing the hand.

Then they returned to the house, and explained to the unconscious merrymakers that Jerry had had an accident. There was consternation and concern for five minutes. Then they filled the jug again.

That was all. But the kiss that Kathleen gave him as she went indoors that night soothed all the pain that Jerry had suffered.

Next morning he went away, and Kathleen, by the aid of Mary Mulloy, began to make her wedding dress. For of course, in Her Majesty's army there was no room for a maimed man, and Jerry received his discharge, after sundry inquiries from his superiors, to whom he explained stolidly that he had severed his finger with an axe while chopping firewood for his mother. As they could not make more out of it than this, they charitably assumed that he was drunk when the accident happened, and let him go.

And when, a few days later, Jerry M'Carthy came again through the Fold, shorn of his military garments, and arrayed as an ordinary and respectable civilian, the folk came hastily to their doors to shout out a welcome to the Irish lad; for the tale had gone throughout the Fold, and had been expounded on every doorstep for days and nights together. Such an act of daring heroism had never been known before, and that a man should cut off his finger just for the sake of a girl was regarded as a half incredible miracle. Indeed, one of the gossips ran to meet him, craftily clutched his maimed hand, and then ran back shouting: "It's a God's trooth. 'E's cut it off. I've seen 'is 'and."

So they all welcomed him home, though Old Benny Rowen, whose patriotic instincts were strong, refused to see any merit in Jerry's action, and told a story of a doctor whom he knew—"an Englishmun, mind yer,"—who scratched his finger while assisting at a *post-mortem*. "An a scratch from a dead body means certain death," said Benny, impressively, "for morstifikashun sets in, an' yer dead in twenty-fore hours. But this doctor took his knife out, an' he whittled the flesh off his finger where he'd bin scratched, just the same as you or me might a piece o' wood"— and Benny held out his finger and shuddered impressively. " 'E cut the flesh off his finger in bits, an' stopped the pison from spreddin', and find me an Irishman with pluck enough t' do that," concluded the old man, scornfully.

But the gossip died away. Jerry went back to his old work, and within a month he and Kathleen Crone were married.

And Mary Mulloy danced at their wedding.

THE COMING AND GOING OF DENIS REGAN

Marriages are commonly said to be made in heaven, but the dwellers on this earth set little store on divine gifts, and in the using commonly abuse them carelessly and callously till all trace of their origin is for ever effaced.

For the first few weeks the married life of Jerry and Kathleen M'Carthy was so happy that even the children looked enviously upon them as they strolled arm-in-arm through, and away from, the Fold every night, after the day's work was done. And even the old folk, whose eyes held the sombre cynicism that comes naturally to travellers who all their lives have journeyed homewards along the gutters, blinded on summer days by the pungent dust, and soddened and spattered on wet and wintry days by the filth under their feet and the mud whirled at their faces from the wheels of the carriages that roll their respectable prisoners along to the same destination—these looked on and were silent, save for a look of tragic anticipation which crossed their faces or centred itself within their shadowed eyes.

They had made good resolutions, these two; to be steady and temperate; never to quarrel; to be clean and thrifty; and in good and bad times to be all-in-all to each other. Instinctively they felt that if they remained too much among the old surroundings they would simply become as the others. So, dressed in their Sunday best, night after night they walked through the streets or away to the fields, returning late, but never too late to find Irish Row seated on its doorsteps, with the inevitable pint jug to every group.

But youth—strong, healthy, and lusty youth —craves variety; and there was not much variety in this. And by and bye they became used to it all; and when the dark nights came on, and Jerry's work grew slack, and their Sunday finery became shabby, it began to get monotonous. And the great curse of life, the worst of all bad habits, the vilest of all vices, is monotony. Within it, since the beginning, have been buried the hopes and ideals of unnumbered souls, and for these there is no resurrection. Take a man out of his rut, and set him on his feet in the middle of the road, and by and bye he will begin to shift for himself. But set him again in the place whence he came, and he will at once begin crawling, as though he had never been away from his rut; and there he will stay, unless you release him again.

And so it was with these two. Gradually, unconsciously, they fell back into the shadows from which they had emerged to bask and make love in the sunshine of a few glorious summer days. And perhaps they were more at home in the shadows.

Jerry became just as he was before he went away, shiftless and occasionally intemperate; but he developed a tendency to recklessly increase the occasions, now that he had a wife to keep on a wage that was never sufficient to keep himself in decency. And Kathleen went just the same road; lost her clean, tidy ways and fell into the slatternly, coarse habits of the women about her; joined in the nightly drinking, till her eyes were as dull and her brain as sluggish as theirs; and quarrelled fiercely with her man whenever existence grew too monotonous—which happened at least once a week.

And two years later, nobody seeing them would ever have suspected or dreamed that such a pitiful, paltry, married life had had such a romantic beginning. Sometimes, on nights when money—and therefore beer—was scarce, they would be something like the couple of old; but that was seldom, only when Mary Mulloy came in to read her last letter from Denis Regan, whose home-coming seemed still as far away as ever.

But one day, when none expected him, he came; and that night, in the home of Mary Mulloy, there was another great re-union. All the neighbours were there, sitting about on boxes or on the floor in front of the fire, for the only three chairs in the house were occupied by Mary's old mother, Denis Regan and Mary herself, her hand within his arm, and a look of pensive brightness on her waiting, weary face.

The jugs were emptied and filled, and the glasses went round and round; and songs were sung and tales were told, mainly by the others, for Denis had grown quiet and reticent in his travels, and there was ever an alert look in his eyes which caused them to look towards him in some degree of reverence, for Denis had always been clever, and had made his way abroad, and it was known that he had been among the Fenians in New York and elsewhere.

Then, as the hours went on, Jerry grew wordy, and, with a glistening in his eyes and a proudness in his voice, told how he had cheated Her Majesty, in the winning of his wife; while Kathleen looked across at Denis and Mary. There was no expression in her face, but there was something in her eyes which spoke to Denis Regan of fruit that had gone rotten since the tasting, and of a light that had faded in its dawning.

He saw the look, and understood. They had all been reared together, and he and Kathleen were ever good friends; and as he looked in her face his eyes saw beside it her face as it had appeared to him in his dreams during his travels, and the contrast was so foul that as he looked from her to her husband, talking excitedly, with ale-moist eyes and swaggering utterance, a look of sneering contempt crossed his face, and then gave place to one of pitying regret.

It was just an exchange of glances, but Jerry M'Carthy saw the look, and paused ominously. Mary Mulloy saw it, too, and darted a quick, jealous glance upwards, but Regan's face was as expressionless as before. He began to tell a story of his wanderings, and the incident was apparently forgotten. The Irish nature is nothing if not passionate, in hating and avenging as in loving—usually it is hastily and impulsively so. There is danger then, but never one half so much as when a composed and maybe smiling face hides a brain that is brooding on, and tragically retentive of, every detail of some real or fancied wrong.

And so, although for a few weeks things went on just as usual, after the news of Denis Regan's return had ceased to be a subject of gossip, it was apparent to one or two observers that hidden fires were smouldering. Though he accepted the general understanding that he was Mary Mulloy's lover, Denis was not demonstrative when in her presence, and at times seemed more than distant. Her quick sensitive nature felt what seemed to be slights, and night after night as she watched him laughing and talking gaily with Kathleen M'Carthy there was a waiting glare in her eyes that hardly passed when Denis kissed her at parting.

Every night the four sat together, while old Mrs. Mulloy sat in her corner, and drank intermittently from her glass as she listened to their talk. Denis had returned with plenty of money, and spent it freely. He never allowed Jerry's glass to remain empty, and as Jerry talked and gabbled glibly under the influence he never caught the sneer on the other man's face, nor did Denis catch the gleam in the eyes of the girl who watched him as he seemed to be making love to another man's wife.

This could not last long. The tension was too great for one woman. One night, as Jerry had paused in a tale to take up his glass, he saw a look in Mary's eyes which stayed his hand, and caused him to glance across the room where his Kathleen and Denis were whispering together. He emptied his glass steadily enough, but the devil came into his eyes as he looked again and saw the same thing, and Mary shuddered, seeing dimly what she had invoked.

That night, clinging passionately to his arm, she whispered something to Denis, and for some days he was seldom with the M'Carthys, and went about with Mary so much that the light came back to her eyes.

Then Easter came. Work had been good, so the Sunday clothes were released from a long stay in the pawnshop, and Jerry and Kathleen, arrayed in their best, looked something like the lovers of old.

Now in that part of Staffordshire, Easter Monday is known as "Heaving Day." A man who can steal behind a woman, clasp his arms round her waist, and heave her bodily from the ground, can claim forfeit-in the shape of a kiss, or, what is more usual and popular, the price of drinks round. On the Tuesday the women have the heaving privilege.

Early on this morning, as all in Irish Row were at their doors, Denis adroitly pinioned Kathleen and lifted her from the ground. He claimed the kiss, which was given freely. Jerry glared stealthily, then vengefully caught Mary, who slapped his face as he tried to kiss her. And the kiss and the blow were both remembered, though he laughed it off lightly enough. All day long there was revelry in Irish Row, and the Spotted Dog had a good day. At night there was a houseful in Mulloy's. Denis had invited all the neighbours, and of whisky and ale there was a store.

At first Jerry and his wife sat together. Later in the evening Denis beckoned to her and gave her a full glass. She drank, and at a touch from him, sat by his side. At the same moment Jerry lifted his glass and emptied it. It was ale. His next was whisky, and this he emptied at a gulp.

Now it is a bad thing for an excitable man to drink intoxicants at all. It is worse if he drinks hastily and often. If he be drinking beer, well and good—to some extent—but if he be drinking beer and whisky, and Irish whisky, nearly neat at that, then pity those in his company.

Denis had never been so free and gay as he was that night. He had been drinking a little more than usual, and that may have caused it. He told stories and sang songs, and laughed and jested with the woman at his side, never seeing the man who was watching them both with a crafty, wild furtiveness in his eyes.

Suddenly Jerry made a movement as if to speak, and as suddenly Denis exclaimed curtly, "Sit down. Kathleen is goin' to sing—for me."

Jerry sat back in his chair, gripping the seat fiercely. Kathleen sang, in a voice almost as sweet as it had been in her girlhood, that sweet and touching song of Le Fanu's, which had been taught her by one of the nuns in the old convent school.

"THE RIVER RAN BETWEEN THEM.

"The river ran between them,
  And she gazed upon the stream;
And the soldier looked upon her
  As a dreamer on a dream.
    'Believe me, oh believe,'
    He cried, 'You peerless maid;
    For my honour is pure,
    And my true love sure,
    Like the white plume in my hat
    And my shining blade.'

"The river ran between them,
  And she smiled upon the stream;
And the soldier looked upon her
  As a dreamer on a dream.
    'I will not trust your promise,
    I will not be betrayed;
    For your faith is light
    And your cold wit bright
    As the white plume in your hat
    And your shining blade.'

"The river ran between them,
  And he rode beside the stream;
And he turned away and parted
  As a dreamer from his dream.
    And his comrade brought his message
    From the field where he was laid;

> Just his name to repeat,
> And to lay at her feet
> The white plume from his hat
> And his shining blade."

There was a solemn hush in the old kitchen as she ended, and a strange glistening in many eyes. Then, somehow, it happened that Denis stooped over the singer and kissed her, and Mary Mulloy clutched his arm with the pain that had gone to her heart, while Jerry M'Carthy, with hell in his hating eyes, jumped up, swinging the glasses from the table with his coat laps as he did so. He faced the two; Kathleen laughing in quizzing defiance, and Denis with the old contemptuous sneer on his face.

"An' is it you that calls yerself a man, to be after makin' love to another man's wife, an' that before his eyes, you dirty, fornicating——" Jerry paused, then spat out venomously, "foreigner."

Denis struck him and he fell. There was wild uproar at once. Jerry scrambled to his feet, snatched a jug from the table, and threw it—not at Denis—malevolently, murderously, full in Kathleen's face. It smashed on her forehead, and she rolled on the floor. Then he rushed at Denis, who felled him again. But he was on his feet in a second, snatched something from the table, and rushed at his enemy, who stood waiting. The women rushed between. In the scuffle Denis was thrown off his guard—Jerry saw it—and with crafty ferocity ran forward and struck him full in his chest. There was a knife in his hand, and Denis fell this time.

And as the door was thrown open, and the women rushed shrieking into the crowd that, hearing the row, had gathered in the alley, the children, who had edged themselves right in front of all, saw Kathleen lying bleeding near the fire, her mother staunching the wound in her forehead. In the middle of the kitchen, on the bare floor, lay Denis Regan, dying, and over him stood Jerry M'Carthy, staring downward in dizzy terror.

Mary, kneeling by her lover's side, looked up at his murderer in a frenzy of speechless horror. In his fall, Denis had clutched her hand, and it was in her eyes that he looked even as he died.

And Jerry, sobered and appalled, saw it, wherefore he turned his head; he dared not look in her face.

.   .   .   .   .

And that is why the folk in Irish Row dwelt

apart from the others, and the children of Tumblefold never entered that passage after dark, and only in hurrying groups by daylight.

CHAPTER XVI

A SUNDAY EVENING SERVICE

I SAT a-thinking, shadowed by the long white window curtains from the steadfast glow of the sun that was kissing lingeringly the far-away verge of the sea, whose listless, lapping wavelets I had been watching all the evening. And as I sat I became conscious of a sudden withdrawal of the living sunlight, which was as suddenly and as strangely replaced by the cold and phosphorescent glimmer of a long, long buried yesterday: a glimmer which was neither twilight nor moonlight, but had all the eerie foreboding of the one and the sense of hopeless isolation which the other always brings. At the same time I felt pressing upon my brain the old dread of unyielding limitations, and the stupefying consciousness of immurement in a catacomb prison, with which I have awakened many a night in terror so intense that I have strained my ears to listen till the familiar boom of the waves beating steadily against the cliffs has brought re-assurance to me. And this time there was no escape; though instinctively I stretched out my hands, the glamour of that sunset slipped away, and I found myself in Tumblefold, lonely amid loneliness; pressing against a door which had never yet been opened, and waiting, waiting.

·   ·   ·   ·   ·

"It's a bloomin' shame, yes it is," said Willie Potter, "and I'd like ter——"

"And I would," said Ryder, savagely.

"You shut up," said Potter; "what you gassin' at? Can't yer wait till I've finished?"

"——ter punch 'is big 'ed till the blood come," ended Ryder, without noticing the rebuke.

"Sh-h-h, that's wicked," said Freddy Stubbs.

"I don't care if it is," said Ryder, defiantly. Then, in weak extenuation: "But it ain't. 'Tain't in the Commandments, is it?" He went on, dimly conscious that his case had failed: "Besides, what right's 'e got to turn us out? S'pose we 'ave got ragged cloase, 'tain't our fault, is it? An' ain't we as good as anybody else is? Don't the Bible say so? Besides, I didn't pull the bloomin' bell."

There was no reply, and for a time the five of us stood moodily together under our window, looking down the main square at the Others who were playing and singing merrily at the opposite end, outside the Spotted Dog. For our feelings were sorely hurt. Living, as we did, in the respectable end of the Fold, we always carried with us the consciousness that we were not quite so low as the Others. And the duties which followed on that consciousness, though irksome and unpalatable, we usually fulfilled. We cleaned our boots on Sunday mornings, went to a Church Sunday school at least once during the day, and refrained from playing any games more irreligious than racing in bare feet, or "nake," a variety of hide-and-seek, in which all hid themselves in alleys and passages, leaving one at the corner of our house, who named them as he caught them peeping out or running across.

But the Others, not so refined, and certainly not so respectable as we, took no account of Sunday, and played marbles, tipcat, football, and even pitch-and-toss, just the same as usual.

Not far away from the Fold was a little mission church, which for some time we had been in the habit of attending on Sunday nights. We were only street lads, and simple as the service was, comprehended nothing of the faith as taught by the square-featured old

mission preacher, though we were staunch
adherents of the Anglican creed, as all Church-
taught children are.

But the singing of the hymns, mostly from
Moody and Sankey, the strange quietness during prayers, and the haunting awe which in
such places falls on those to whom most things,
material and immaterial, are hopelessly inscrutable, always thrilled to that hidden sense
of nearness to the Invisible which lies at the
heart of all humanity.

And when, in that place, and under that
sombre glamour, we were told to "order ourselves lowly and reverently to all our betters,"
and to "do our duty in that state of life to
which it had pleased God to call us," we accepted the insinuations of unfitness, and leaned
back into the shadows to avoid being seen, as
we sat in a row on a long wooden bench at
the back of the room.

This was our seat for many weeks, till one
Sunday night some of the Others suddenly
grew concerned for their own spiritual wel-
fare, and followed us into the room. They
were sheepish enough at first.

But—they had never been under the influence, and by-and-bye they grew restless. From
the ceiling to the seat of our bench hung the
rope of the bell which called the worshippers
to the service. We had never meddled with

it; but one of the Others saw it, and furtively felt for the end of the rope. And just as the missioner was giving out his text, there was a tug at the rope, a jarring brazen note that made everybody look round, while the missioner stared indignantly at the doorkeeper, who rose wrathfully and hustled us all out.

The Others laughed greatly over the joke, but we went home ashamed and humiliated. And the next Sunday night, when we presented ourselves, we were not astonished when the doorkeeper met us in the passage and savagely exclaimed: "Now, ger out o' this, ye dirty ragamuffins. D'y'ear what I say? Hook it, and don't y'ever come 'ere again. If yer do, I'll——!"

And so we went back to the Fold, and gathered moodily under our window, while the Others called out banteringly from a distance: "Look who's got chucked out o' the mission-room."

We were angry and downhearted. Poor little slum-shadowed pariahs as we were, in all our darkness there had still been with us the belief that outside and above all others was One in whom we could trust, albeit His way seemed often crooked and sinister even to us with our unquestioning faith. The assurance that some day He would make it all right had kept us straight many and many a time, and the knowledge that, however ragged and despised we might be, in His house we were equal with others, although we did sit on the back seat, had been wonderfully comforting to us.

And now, even from His house we had been turned away, maybe while He was looking on; and conscious that our last hope had somehow been ruthlessly snatched from us, we stared savagely down at the Others, half hoping they would come just near enough to challenge a fight.

After Ryder's outbreak we were silent for some time. Then Willie Potter burst out again: "It's all rot. That's wot it is. It ain't a bit o' use tryin' to be good. It don't make no difference. God don't know anythin' about it, an' if He does He don't care anythin' about us. Let's 'ave a go at football. I don't believe," he concluded, with an effort at bravado which palpably failed, "that there *is* a God."

Potter's father was an Atheist, and had even argued with the Vicar once; but Willie had always opposed his parent, much to his amusement. So this assertion was terrible, and little Freddie Stubbs said, intreatingly, "Willie, yer don't mean it, do yer?"

And Ryder promptly exclaimed, "You'll go into the burning pit for that, Willie Potter. I shouldn't be surprised if the devil wasn't standing behind yer now—waitin'."

Potter turned pale and looked round quickly. Then, with a feeble laugh, he said: "Of course, I didn't mean it. I was only coddin', wasn't I?" and he looked appealingly round. Of course, we all said "yes," and, somewhat reassured, he remarked, "But it's a bloomin' shame, an' it ain't hardly right as we should be turned out for doin' nothin'."

"I tell y'r what," said Jones, "let's get some hymn-books an' sing some hymns. It'll be better than nothin'."

"Right," said Potter quickly, still full of remorse for his blasphemy, "an' perhaps that'll make it all right."

So each rummaged for hymn-books, and we sat together on the hard stones under our window. And by-and-bye Nellie Joyce and Maggie Lawley came and sat near, and Teddy Wall hobbled up on his crutches; and one by one some of the Others came up till nearly a score of children were huddled together. At first the Others were inclined to treat the whole thing as a joke, but gradually the mysterious influence of the melodies overcame, and in a short time on every sallow face, and in all their sunken, sombre eyes was a faint glimmer of the faith-reflected glory of the world beyond.

And so we sang through the twilight, while in Irish Row they laughed and danced, and from the Spotted Dog came lusty choruses which jarred harshly with the lingering hymn refrains. But though the folk looked on indifferently from their doorsteps, and those passing to and from "The Dog" stared at the ragged, reverent group, we continued our service unmolested, singing hymns we had learned at Sunday School, snatches of others we had heard the missioners sing—"There's a Friend for little children," "I think when I read," "There is a happy land," "Tell me the old, old story"—all other-worldly, and bright with a promise that this had never known. Of this world we had already had our experiences, like the melancholy Jacques, and, like his, they had been none too pleasing or pleasant.

So the children sang of angels' voices, with the blasphemous Babel of the Spotted Dog smoke-room in their ears; of being "washed whiter than snow," their faces thin and yellow with foul air, and their bodies wasted through lack of food; of "scattering seeds of kindness," while the seeds of misery, drudgery, immorality, and disease had already been sown amongst them; of "gathering at the river," while through the stagnant filth of weeks the afternoon's rain trickled down the gutter in Tumblefold; of a "home eternal," while they were never sure of their own for more than a fortnight at a stretch; of being "clad in robes of white," while the lads were clothed in rags,

and wore odd boots with or without soles, and
the girls wore torn and dirty frocks, few with
more than a patchwork skirt under them, and
boots that had been sorted from marine stores;
of a Great Physician always near, while Teddy
Wall was a hopeless cripple through spinal
curvature, and scarcely one but bore in his or
her stunted body the germs of debility, consumption, or some other disease from the
varied stock which the children of Tumblefold
inherited—and they ended by singing "Marching to Zion"—*via* Tumblefold, the gaol, and
the workhouse.

*And God saw everything that He had made;
and behold, it was very good!*

It was quite dark, and no stars were out, as
Potter's father stumbled towards us from the
Spotted Dog just as we had started on the
last hymn.

He stopped short, with a look of cunning
knowledge in his beer-dulled eyes.

"Don't you believe it," said he, lurching into
the group that sat in the darkness. "You

listen to me, little 'uns. When yer teachers an' yer parsons come an' tell yer there's a good God above as made all, an' give carriages an' money—any amount of money to some, an' nothin' but poverty an' rags, an' hard work, an' blue-splashed little money, an' mighty little beer"—this with a drunken chuckle—"to others, tell 'em they're liars. There ain't any God at all, an' if there is He ought to be ashamed o' Hissel' for servin' us as He has done."

He lurched away, while the children stared uneasily at each other and the great blackness above.

Freddie's voice broke the silence. "Let's finish it off like a proper meetin'—who'll say a prayer?"

All eyes turned on Willie Potter, who, mindful of his recent error, accepted the implied though silent obligation. He stood up with hands folded, as he had seen the mission preachers stand, then took off his ragged cap, through a rent in which a tuft of his curly hair was always peeping.

"Our—you tek y'r hat off, Ryder, an' you, Billy Wilde, an' you little 'uns. This is real, ye know—we ain't coddin'—Our Father, which art in heaven, I—I—we—please we're only a lot of little lads an' gels what lives in Tumblefold, an' we *do* want to be all right, an' we've been to the mission-room many times, an' we went to-night, an' ol' Johnny Harris chucked us all out, an' said we was dirty ragamuffins, an' please, Lord, it ain't our fault, an' it *is* 'ard lines on us 'cause we can't help bein' bad off, an' we want to keep all right, only ol' Johnny Harris won't let us in. We know we ain't wot we orterbe, but look where we live an' wot we 'ave to put up with, an'—an'—an'—please, Lord, *do* give us a chance—give us a chance—an' we'll come out all right. Amen."

He ended abruptly, while an admiring whisper went round, "Ain't he a knock-out? He'll be a bloomin' parson, 'e will, yet."

There was a dead silence. In the darkness they sat with their eyes staring forward with that unseeing stare which betrays deep and solemn reflection. The moon, which had been hidden nearly all the night, came out suddenly and kissed the foreheads of the children in pity, since they, like her, were doomed to death in life.

In the eyes of little Stubbs there was a strange glistening as he stared down towards the door through which we had peered on the night when Irish Katie left us. He saw not the bare shanty but the Gates of which we had been singing. The others saw only the darkness and the light which died as Stubbs fell in meditation, and his eyes grew dull again.

So we sat a-thinking, till a sudden uproar betokened "turning-out-time" at the Spotted Dog, and we hurried down to see the fights.

.   .   .   .   .

And as my eyes looked once more in recognition on the shimmering sea which lapped the hulking at the end of the street, I thought bitterly of that unanswered prayer. Yet in a world whose every revolution is a mighty, yet apparently unnoticed straining towards its Guide, of what avail could be the prayer of one poor little maggot unit?

Yet was it cruel all the same, for though it was given to one or two to escape, the others were left in their den till they grew as dull and heavy and hopeless as the walls in their prison, the stones of its pavement, and the firmament figment above them.

And I, who am one that escaped—I, who now write with a pen dipped in the corroding ink of a poisonous past—because I cannot, will not, dare not forget or forgive the wrongs that were heaped by God and men upon me and on those who are wallowing to-day in Tumble-fold, and on those who have found at least rest—they could find no more loathsome, no fouler darkness—in the clay pits in the cemetery—I am by respectable people shunned as an enemy of society.

Well, let it be so. Perhaps it is just as well.

CHAPTER XVII

FEVER

SUMMER was always a trying time for the little children. The bigger ones were privileged: they could journey whither they willed in quest of fresh air and pleasure, and, providing they got into no trouble when out, might stay as long as they chose. But the little ones were confined to the many "ins" and fewer "outs" of the Fold. They could run or hide in the dark passages, many not a yard wide, or in the main passages play hop, stride, and a jump from gutter to gutter. If through the summer they caught nothing from the smells, they were counted healthy; the insurance fees were unwillingly paid, or allowed to lapse.

The smells were an important institution in Tumblefold. The gutters were never swilled, except by the rain, and that was made filthy as it came through the foul atmosphere of the Fold.

Many houses were dirty all through, and stank horribly. In the same room were stored the family food and the family refuse, to say nothing of the dirty clothes piled up against washing day. In the gutter fronting every house was always a miscellaneous heap of potato peelings, fish heads and entrails, and other garbage, remaining there usually till the rain swept it down. On this putrid mixture the sun fell every morning, and round it the children played, breathing in the smells with open mouths.

Smells have a closer connection with life than many people would think. The nose is not the least important part of a man's face. Usually it plays for the body the same detective part that the eyes do, or should do, for the mind. How many mortal antipathies have been caused by a mere smell; how many affinities owe their beginnings to the same trivial cause? The faintest sniff of an onion has marred many a kiss, and maybe hindered not a few engagements. How many men have lost their heads and their hearts at the same moment, through the smell of a rose in a girl's bosom, or the delicate perfume on her dress, coupled with the rare and indescribable sensation caused by contact with a body in perfect physical health and cleanliness?

From infancy I have always been strangely

susceptible to smells, and even after a lapse of years the sudden recurrence of an old-time odour has roused memories that have slept till almost forgotten.

Sometimes, in passing a joiner's shop, I breathe the odour of deal shavings, and I lose myself for a moment in the past. I see a long shed on the edge of a dark waste of pit mounds and cinder heaps. It is a wheelwright's shop. Wheels, hubs, old shafts and bodies, are scattered about.

Inside is a tall, gaunt old man. His face is strong, his chin is heavy and resolute. It is a giant's head—a giant undeveloped. He planes steadily the plank before him, and his eyes light up with pleasure as he turns to an ill-clad, white-faced lad beside him, asking or answering many questions. They are grandsire and grandson. The lad has brought the old man's dinner. They are close friends. The one is clever at his books, and the old man is proud of him. Being of inquisitive bent he gets a full account of the morning lessons, all about grammar, geography, and the stories in the reading book.

The lad learns lessons, too, as he watches the strong hands at work, planing, screwing, and fitting,—or steadily driving nails, always hitting the nail plump on the head. How he admires the strength and dexterity of the man, who, in his turn, reveres what is to him the deep knowledge of the boy, and dreams wistfully of what might have been had he had the same opportunities. The lad runs away to school, with a penny in his pocket to buy a book with. All afternoon his schoolmates are sniffing the odour of the shavings he has rolled in.

Years have come and gone since then. The old workshop is gone, too, and the old wheelwright. Perhaps he is learning now all that he missed before, and is sturdily availing himself of the opportunities that were never given him here. But the lad remains; a lad no longer; and would give up many dreams just to shake the hard hands of his grandfather and look in the worn old face once more.

There is another smell which I hate, that of burning pitch. It recalls to me that old house in the Fold, with pitch burning on the stairs and in one dark room, with ceiling and walls damp and dingy. In this room, on a low bed, is being held down by force a man in dying agony, blasphemous, but happily delirious. Kneeling at his side is a woman crying and praying. This is what met the view of a terrified child, who had crept upstairs and peered into the room.

At odd moments, unaccountably, comes a pleasanter odour, the strong life-and-laughter-

giving odour of the sea. Then I renew my
youth.

It is my first holiday in five-and-twenty
years. A sunny August morning. I and
another are walking briskly down a mountain
path in North Wales. Mountains surround
us, and a merry little stream follows the course
of the path. To me, for the first time away
from the desolate blackness of Wolverhampton, it is all so beautiful that I could cry aloud
for joy. A few minutes later I do so. A
sudden odour meets me, so strong and potent
that for a second it snatches my breath; then
I inhale it in long, deep breaths. It is the
sea, a mile away, and not yet visible.

We turn a corner. I see in the distance,
high between two mountains, a glittering
stretch of darkness lit by sunlight, and
covered with what seem to me to be countless
white-breasted birds. Then, as my eyes grow
used to it, I see that the white-breasted birds
are waves and the glittering stretch of glory
is the sea.

"The commensurate antagonist of all the earth."

These are digressions, I admit, but I have
not, I think, been very egotistical so far. In
fact, I could not very well be so. The others
were far in front of me, and the lines which
follow tell of the only, and that not exciting,

incident which I gave to the story of our friendship.

It had been a very hot summer from its beginning. It was whispered in Tumblefold that the cholera was sure to come this time, and fearful tales were told of the last visitation by some who remembered it. But the gutters were kept no cleaner.

One night we saw a closed carriage roll down and stop before a dirty house. A little girl was brought out, and taken away. It was a very bad case, and she never came back.

That was the beginning. Next morning came a man with a disinfecting utensil, with which he went over the house and its inmates; even stopping as he came past our group to disinfect us, much to our surprise. The smell of that disinfectant never left Tumblefold that summer, and to me it is still one of the most vivid sensations I know.

Next night the carriage came again, this time taking two children, and next night it came for two more. It was scarlet fever, and had gained a very strong hold. We five were forbidden to mix with the others, and played anywhere but in Tumblefold.

The terror continued, and at the end hardly a house remained that the carriage had not visited. The drains were cleansed daily now, but it was too late. Death had made almost

a house-to-house visitation. One day I was
ill, and could not go to school. My head was
bad, my throat was worse, and I was so sick
that I could not eat. In the afternoon I
crawled upstairs and lay down. When I
awoke it seemed dark, I felt myself choking,
and on looking at the clock I saw with horror
that I could not tell the time, although I saw
the face and the fingers distinctly. I stumbled
downstairs; and my face, I suppose, was
enough. There were queer looks exchanged,
and I was marched to the doctor's.

We sat waiting, and the others in the room
gave me the same queer look. Some of them
moved away.

Our turn came; I went in the little room
trembling. The doctor gave me the same
quick look, asked a few questions, then called
my mother aside. She beckoned me out, but
that was not to my mind. I wanted to know,
and said to the doctor, "Please, sir, what
is it?"

He was astonished, but after another scru-
tiny, said, "It's scarlet-fever-sore-throat, and
you'll have to be very good, and take your
medicine, and do just as I tell you."

That was bad, but I had another question,
"Please, sir, is it—is it dangerous?"

I had a morbid horror of death, and another
doctor might have caused it. This one, how-

ever, was a man, and said, "It isn't so *very* bad, yet, but you must be good, and go to bed and don't get up or have anything to eat till I tell you. You trust to me."

With a kindly pat on the head he dismissed me. That night, and for many days and nights after, I was very ill. After a struggle with the authorities I was allowed to remain at home, our house being clean and comfortable.

I was an exemplary patient. I had faith in the doctor's word that I had caught nothing more serious than scarlet-fever-sore-throat, and would get better. So I took my medicine and lay still. It was a miserable time. My brain was busy and weary all the while. The worst feeling was that I was such a wretched outcast. No other children were allowed near me, and my own kin were too busy to sit much with me. And for a child to be shorn of talk, of motion, and laughter is a fearful thing.

I used to lie awake all day thinking of the strangest things, but always resigned to my lot. It was just a matter of patient waiting, that was all. I submitted to the periodical garglings, but I could not make out why every cup I used should be so carefully washed. What had I done? Was I poisonous?

Every noon I had one question to ask, "Does the doctor say I can get up to-day?"

"No—not to-day."

"To-morrow?"

"No—not to-morrow."

"When?"

"Lie still and go to sleep. Only a day or so, now."

So the weeks went on. I had no feeling of weakness, and all along felt able to walk about. Once I got out of bed, and tried to walk. To my utter surprise I fell in a heap, and was too much astonished to heed the scolding I got.

I was forbidden to eat, though after the first week my appetite was voracious. The doctor's word was law, so I starved. I had one solace. I was very fond of jam tarts, and nothing would satisfy me till two penny tarts were bought and placed on a shelf where I could see them all day. I used to watch those tarts for hours, licking my lips at the prospective reward of virtuous resignation; and tickling my palate with epicurean thoughts of the pleasure to come.

Reading had no charms for me, picture books no pleasure. I was tired all the time, till night came. Then my brain began to work, and toiled industriously till dawn at the most improbable tasks. I was in school, snowballing, and playing football, getting caned for bad lessons, kicked in the games, and struck by stones instead of snowballs, all in the space of a minute. Always in the distance were the shadowy figures of my four chums, strangers now, with little Stubbs in the middle beckoning wistfully—always I called to them, and heard no reply.

I had fitful dreams, each one an incarnation of one or other of my childish dreads. I was buried alive, was drowned, was threatened by hideous demon faces; sometimes I was lost on a great wet waste, wherein I sank to my knees, and putrid smells would rise till I awoke, choking. And there was the dread, which would come in spite of the doctor's assurance, of a change for the worse, and the final horror, death.

It was a hard time for me, but I pulled through it. My four chums made daily inquiries, and night after night I heard their voices under the window below. How, I longed to be with them! One morning I heard a shout. It was Jones: "Johnny! Johnny Yeubrey!"

Then, knowing there could be no reply, Ryder yelled: "School's broke up! Three weeks' holiday! Hoo-ray!"

They meant well, but I turned over and cried.

They were true to our bond, and day after day went long walks, bringing back colossal bunches of flowers, which brightened the room wonderfully. They took turns to shout up all the news of the Fold and the day's adventures, taking for granted that I heard and was interested, as indeed I was. At night they stood under the window singing our school songs, and finishing with the Christmas chorus. I enjoyed it, but the unfeeling neighbours rebelled, and put a sudden end to the juvenile serenades.

When I was well enough to stand by the window and talk down to them our joy was great. We discussed what we should do when I was better; and games and walks were carefully planned. With curious reticence they never spoke of the other children. I knew the reason as I looked down the Fold. It was swept clean, and was always very quiet. The children seemed almost to have deserted it.

At last I was free, and when I was used to my feet, we took a walk. Arm in arm we went, I in the middle, till we came to a field, and lay down on the grass, plucking it by handfuls, and talking intermittently. We were five once more.

Gradually I learned how few of the children who went away in the carriage had returned, and how many had gone away, for ever and for ever. And as we recalled memories of games with one or other of the dead children, forgetting past foolishness and thinking of the best and sunniest sides of their natures, in one heart at least was a silent thankfulness that the links had not been broken which held us five together.

CHAPTER XVIII

HOW THE CHILDREN WENT A-MAYING

MANY moons passed before the tale of the journey to find the King's Palace and the Garden had ceased to be told at nights to wondering clusters of the little ones.

As the first sight and smell of the sea breathe into a man's life a longing that never leaves him, so that receding afternoon, with its glimpses of budding hedges and fields growing green at the bidding of the sun that smiled and the birds that sang, became a paradise in Time, towards whose barred gates those little lads gazed in health-seeking instinct in their dreams; when their eyes were darkening and their hearts were flagging with the gutter-exhaled air, and the misery, stabbing and pitiless as an east wind in March, which made their lair in Tumblefold.

In a world like this, it is something to be thankful for that we never forget our pleasant dreams, and that while the fiercest physical pain is numbed in the healing halls of memory, it is given to us by an unknown justice—blind, maybe, but justice nevertheless—to recall every throb and every ray of past happiness and sunshine.

These lads lived through many moonless nights and dull drab days; but nothing could rob them of the store of joy which was caverned in their hearts. To the younger children they were as travellers, whose journey into a far country had invested them with strange glamour. And they listened to the ever-fresh tale of the journey in silent awe, fearing to breathe audibly, lest capricious dignity should cut short the tale, and disperse the audience.

But one night, when Willie Potter had ended the story, he brought a new light into their eyes by magnanimously promising to lead the way to the fields some day in the summer, if all the children in the Fold that could walk, and were not afraid of bobbies, would make up their minds to go.

That was a year or two after the first adventure.

The offer was hailed with delight, and the excited children were discussing when and where to go, when Nelly Joyce exclaimed:

"Why, it's first Sunday in May neks Sunday. Let's all goo a-Mayin'!"

The children shouted, and pulled at Nelly's pinafore. Potter looked round savagely at the fickle ones who had deserted him for another. But the other was Nellie Joyce, and he smiled affably. He had spent all his pocket money (a penny a week) on several occasions in buying sweets for her. She always accepted and shared them with him, a favour she did not confer on other admirers who bought her sweets.

There was a vague superstition in Tumblefold about going a-Maying, and the first Sunday in the merry month was the recognised annual holiday of many of the Folders. Led by some hidden instinct, they went out in the morning away "into the country," vaguely and aimlessly wandering, most of them seeking only to see the green grass and breathe fresh and smokeless air.

Others, in full work, clubbed together and hired a conveyance of some kind for a matter of five shillings, and went further away— to some picturesque old-world village—returning home in clattering state at night, laden with flowers and beer, and singing snatches of songs as they climbed down from their equipage, while the children gathered round and stared at the lathering horses.

This they called going a-Maying, though the May was seldom out so early in the month;

yet if they gathered but a blossoming branch they were well content.

What more natural, then, that the children should desire to go a-Maying, too?

The first of May was on the Saturday, and in the morning a number of the children, following an old custom whose origin none could remember, went a May-poling through the Fold. Nelly Joyce was Queen, decked in tissue-paper garments of many colours, and a tissue-paper crown upon her head; a number of smaller girls were her handmaidens, and a little lad held up proudly a "kissing bush," which served as the Maypole.

The motley and coloured procession went to every house; Nelly stood in the middle, while the others ambled sheepishly round her, singing:

"All around the Maypole
We will trot,
From the very bottom
To the very top.
Now I've got my fancy
To trundle on my knee;
Oh, my lovely Nancy,
She's the girl for me.
She hops and she skips,
While the fiddle does play,
Around the merry, merry Maypole.

First come buttercups,
And then come daisies,
And then come gentlemen,
And then come ladies.
Come shake the box,
Come shake the box,
Will you please to put a copper in?"

The folk whose children took part in the Maypoling, and, indeed, all the others, looked on with satisfaction and some amount of pride as the gay procession went round.

And the strangers who looked on, and saw nothing but the grotesque in the mixture of ribbons and rags in the children's attire, might have judged less hastily had they thought more deeply. For there was a subtle significance in the beggars' masquerade which brought memories of bygone revels on faraway village greens to this sunless city slum.

Long before night came, the money was spent that the children had gathered during the morning. Those were hard times, and all odd coppers were ruthlessly extracted from the little ones, whose earnings for errands often provided a dinner where otherwise would have been none.

So that night we all stood together under our window, Nelly Joyce, divested of her queenly apparel, but prettier than ever in her neatly-patched frock, in the middle, Potter jealously near her, and the others in an excited group pressing round.

All was excitement and expectation. The great journey of the morrow was the subject of conversation. Potter, whose uncle took him out in the country every Sunday morning, was to be the leader, and had decided on the way to take. All he would say was:

"We're goin' into th' country, I tell yer. You leave me alone. *I* know where we're going. Into the country, where there's nothing but fields and trees, and May trees *everywhere.*"

And the children followed his outstretched finger admiringly, half expecting to see May trees before them—"But I'll tell ye," he said, dropping his voice warningly, "ye'll all 'ave to be careful and keep close together—there's bulls in one o' the fields—*mad* bulls," he said, with wholly unnecessary emphasis, "an' there's a river of water—an' if you ain't careful ye'll all tumble in, and be drownded."

He would say no more, and the prospect of being "drownded" was so dreadful that we all began to talk in whispers, till Nelly Joyce exclaimed, coaxingly, with a toss of her head:

"*I* ain't a bit frightened. Tell us where y'r goin', Willie."

Willie was going to say "No," firmly, but the unstudied, yet tantalising toss of a pretty head, revealing a full, white throat and neck, was his undoing, as the same thing has undone many an older and wiser child, and he said:

"Well, I'll tell *you*, Nelly, but don't tell the others."

"No," said she, with a triumphant little laugh. He whispered to her for some minutes, while the children tittered, and glanced slyly at each other.

And in five minutes they all knew that the Waterbridge Fields was the selected walk. And poor little Samson went indoors wrathfully, while his Delilah called out, cheerily, "Good night, Willie."

Willie banged the door.

But all was forgotten early next afternoon, when some two score children of all ages from four to twelve were marching in a motley procession from Tumblefold, headed by Potter, flushed and warm with the labour of getting all ready.

Just as we were starting came a terrific burst of crying behind us.

It was little Teddy Wall, a cripple from birth, who had never left the Fold save on visits to the hospital. He was the only one left.

"Come on," said Potter; "it's no good his

crying.   He can't walk, an' we can't carry him."

"You shut up," said Nelly Joyce.   "He shall come wi' us."

"Who says?" inquired Willie, loftily.

"*I* say," said Nelly, laughing, and running away.   And in a few minutes she returned, trundling Teddy along in a small wheel-barrow, which she had borrowed from the coal-wharf.   The smile on the cripple's face was good to see.   Potter said nothing, but took hold of the barrow.   And we took it in turns to wheel it.

So the procession of children, whose white thin faces wore an expression of sombre wisdom not born of years, went through the streets of Wolverhampton towards the country, laughing and chattering volubly.   Mourners in coaches, the bearers walking beside the hearses, the hundreds of thoroughly respectable people making their way to the parks or Pleasant Sunday Afternoon Classes—all stared in amazement at the motley pilgrimage; and some who had never before realised the deadly, hellish meaning of the word Poverty, understood it then.   But the children looked at them unenviously, and went on.   And, by-and-bye, we came to a green country lane, with hawthorn just blossoming in the hedges high out of our reach, and at last passed excitedly through the gate that led to the fields.

Eh! what a day was that. Words could not tell of its wild joy; how the children ran, laughing and tumbling, over the green grass, upsetting each other noisily, and staring at intervals with wild eyes at the larks high above, and the great blue and white sweep behind which God was hiding, and maybe watching.

And, by-and-bye, the drowsy sweetness of the pure air overcame, and the whole troop lay about in the grass, talking in whispers, and dreamily observing the wonders about them.

But the time went on. "Get up," cried Potter. "We've *ever* so far to go yet—an' the mad bulls are in the next field."

This was sufficient. Cowering close together, we passed into the next field, Potter shivering in front. We saw the "mad bulls," cows mostly, grazing contentedly about the fields; then with a sudden yell of fear ran helter-skelter across, with imaginary bulls at our heels—never resting till we were safe through the gates and in the next field.

"They nearly had us that time," said Potter, wiping his face; "you wouldn't have known if I hadn't a-spoke."

We came to the waterbridge and saw the little rivulet trickling over its tiny falls, in delight that can only be imagined by a slum-born sightseer. And then came a catastrophe.

Potter, with Nelly at his side, became venturesome, and said there were fish in the water. All necks were immediately craned over the water's edge. Potter was in front, and the sudden involuntary movement of the mass of youngsters sent him on his knees in the water. He yelled out:

"I've tumbled in. Murder—murder—oh, mother."

There was wild uproar at once. The water was only a few inches deep, but to us it was as the ocean itself.

"Hold still a minnit," shouted Jones, pulling off his jacket and vest; "I'm comin'. Ger away from the bank, will yer. He'll be drownded in a minnit. Lend's yer hand, Ryder; and you, Johnny Yeubrey."

Four large stones spanned the brooklet. One of them was under water. Potter had fallen near the other bank, and might have struggled out, but didn't think of it. Jones, Ryder and I stood on the three dry stones, and Jones stretched out his hand to Potter, who was crying.

"Now," said Jones, pulling him up, "put y' feet on that stone, an' we'll *soon* have y' out."

By a great effort Potter was raised, and stepped on the submerged stone. He had on hobnailed boots, and promptly slipped with a loud splash and a louder shriek full length into the water.

He was instantly hauled out, soaked through, and spluttering forth water, with intermittent shrieks of "Oh, mother, I'm drownded."

He was drenched, and on that part of his nether garments which was invisible when he sat down, there was a hopeless, shameless crack.

There was no help for it. The girls went away and stood laughing from a distance, while we took him behind a hedge, stripped him, and hung his clothes on the hedge to dry. There he sat shivering all afternoon, while four of us formed a guard in front of him, Jones turning round from time to time with:

"Are y'r better? You'd ha' bin drownded if I hadn't pulled my jacket and weskut off, you would."

The others went into the next field, and played about in the grass, or wandered along the hedges gathering wild flowers; running frequently to Teddy Wall, who lay contentedly in his barrow near us, with the flowers in their hands, exclaiming:

"Smell these, Teddy, *ain't* they lovely?"

And by the time we were ready for home,

the little cripple was nearly buried in sweetness.

The hours wore on, the sun went down, and in the glamour of the twilight we pulled out our scanty stores from our handkerchiefs or bits of paper, and dined with strange happiness and contentment. Potter's clothes were dry, and he and Jones were the centre of an admiring crowd. To have been nearly drowned was a distinction of which Willie was justly proud.

At last we were ready for home. But Nelly Joyce and Claydabber were missing. Potter looked miserable. And just as we were starting away, thinking they must have gone forward, the missing couple came running breathlessly from a distant field, each carrying a great bough of hawthorn, just in blossom.

It was the first of the year, and the little ones went wild with joy as they crowded round, sniffing the sweet flowers. Then the boughs were broken, and the spoils shared round. The largest piece went to Nelly, who carefully broke the prettiest blossom away, and pinned it to Potter's coat.

Then, with her arm in his, she led the way, and we all went home—tired, but very happy.

And as, in the deepening twilight, we straggled through the streets towards the darkness of Tumblefold, it was something more than the glow of a vanished sun which lit up the wan, worn faces of the children, for it faded not that night, nor for many days and nights after.

Soon the shadowed Fold was bright with flowers, merry with unusual laughter, and echoing with songs, which for once had no mournful, wailing burden. Hand in hand they danced round and about the old buildings, with bunches of hawthorn blossom pinned to shabby coats, or lying on pinched and tiny bosoms, and as the fragrance touched their nostrils they wandered still in green fields and under shady hedges, stood timidly on the edge of a little brook, or chased butterflies recklessly across illimitable reaches of green grass.

That night there were services in all the churches and chapels, and the worshippers went home full of faith in the goodness of God, and inspired almost to benevolence by the brilliance of the sermons. All night long, brakes full of trippers returning home rolled heavily up Susbury Road; but they missed the children who usually darted out from the darkness, and ran behind the brakes, clamouring for pennies.

In one street, not far away, there was a quarrel which ended in murder, and the ambulance with the dead body, and the police with their prisoner, went past the outlet of the Fold, followed by a great and noisy crowd.

But the children, who, in Tumblefold,

were chaunting, unconscious of its bitter irony, "Around the merry, merry Maypole," saw nothing, recked nothing of it at all. For to them this one day and night "were as a thousand years."

CHAPTER XIX

CLAYDABBER'S SISTER

SHE was the pride of Tumblefold, Everybody liked her. The children loved her. So did Claydabber, in his way.

He was a great, hulking lad, with an unspeakable contempt for girls, and his sister was the only girl he was ever known to fight or be friends with. His Christian name was Richard, but we called him Claydabber Dick behind his back, or in his hearing, when at a sufficiently respectable distance, because his father was a bricklayer's labourer.

The general tendencies of the dwellers in Tumblefold were towards evil. Therefore, being mindful of Scripture, the authorities considered that one solitary gas lamp would provide all the light that was needed at night. This lamp was placed at one end of the square, and, under it, we lads played or talked on winter nights. At the opposite end we could see the glimmer of the lamp through the shutters of the little low house wherein Katie lived.

She was a slim, dark-eyed Irish girl, and in years was barely eighteen. Her mother was a cripple, whose years, nay, months, were numbered. Her father was not always in work, and as both were ignorant and improvident, and took as little thought for the morrow as do the generality of their race, a week's idleness for the father meant nothing to eat at the end of the week.

So when she left school, Katie found employment in a factory, and by her small earnings helped to keep the home together. Her mother was helpless, and Katie had to wash, and scrub, and cook the morrow's rude meals every night after coming from the factory. Claydabber helped her in his lumbering way, and scrubbed floors and ran on errands with surly vigour, for he was fond of Katie.

She was a favourite in the Fold, too. She was a true Irish girl, saucy, merry, and free, and had worlds of vivacity in her quizzing black eyes.

Before she went to the factory she was the uncrowned queen of the Fold, headed its games and pastimes, had all the older lads for her sweethearts, and laughed when they fought. Many a night she gathered all the children round her in some dark corner of the Fold, and told for hours at a time all the wonderful stories which her mind, steeped in superstition and romance, could remember or imagine.

When she went to work her time for play was shortened, and only on rare occasions did she join in the old-time games. But as the children played about the labyrinth, by day or night, her quick, firm footsteps, and snatches of some old Irish song, sung with strange sweetness, yet with a mournful, haunting cadence, revealed her nearness long before Katie came in view. It was always "Hallo, Kate," from the lads, and a bantering, laughing rejoinder from the Irish lass.

After flirting with all her devoted followers, she fixed her affections on a sturdy young forgeman, Tommy Turner by name, and alternately teased and coaxed him till he was on the verge of desperation. But trade went slack, he was put on short time, and at last dismissed. He walked about till his last rag was pawned; then, having had quite enough, he enlisted in Her Majesty's service.

Winter came on, and trade grew worse. It was the year of the great frost, which lasted nearly three months, and stopped all the works in Wolverhampton. All day long the streets were full of unemployed men, penniless and hungry. The women starved in their dens, as they always do.

Every morning hundreds of men besieged the Town Hall and the various works; every morning they asked for bread, and were offered stones—to break, at a shilling a day.

They began to threaten at last, and it was rumoured that windows were to be smashed, and shops and bread-vans looted. The authorities grew frightened. Subscription lists were started, and numerous wealthy employers made amends, as public benefactors, for individual sins.

Soup kitchens were opened everywhere, and the daintiest ladies, in a glow of philanthropic ardour, condescended to assist. How their pinched-up bosoms swelled, how their little hearts warmed, and how their cold eyes glistened with consciousness of well-doing as they stood, well-clothed and protected, serving out the soup to the dirty, haggard wretches who clamoured at the doors!

Things were bad in Tumblefold. Nearly all the men were thrown out of work by the frost, and, having made no provision for frosty days, their cupboards were soon empty.

For a week or two there was one resource, the pawnshop. Day after day something was missing in every house—first, the Sunday clothes of those who had them went, then the pawnable part of their every-day attire, then the jewellery, wedding rings, cheap silver rings and brooches; bedclothes, beds, the old Family Bibles, chairs, and pictures, till nearly every house in Tumblefold was as bare as the hard, wind-swept stones outside.

The parson appeared in the Fold for the first time, and wore a complacent smirk, because he was able at last to point out to these wretched people the moral of their wicked, dissolute lives; and the justice and righteousness of the judgment which had fallen upon them. Scripture readers and lady tract distributors came, and gloated openly over the spectacle of the wicked man receiving his reward. The poor wretches listened to them silently, if unwillingly; for the saintly scourges brought tickets for soup, coal, bread, and sometimes small groceries; and the anticipations of these somewhat tempered the wind to the shorn.

The Tumblefold lads were united in misfortune, and forgot their feuds, as they sat at the soup dinner provided for them daily in the schools. There was nothing to eat at home, and one basin of soup a day was for weeks the only food many of them had; but it helped them to face the white terror which held the land in a grip of death.

Claydabber's father was one of the first to

be thrown out; but Katie was in work, and Dick went out selling papers and matches, so they suffered little at first. But in the middle of the frost Katie's work was stopped, and a week later they were starving. Even Dick's paper money was gone. They had nothing pawnable in the house to start with, so they had to beg and borrow till their neighbours were tired, for they too were in the same plight.

One night a group of lads were talking moodily under the gas lamp. Little Stubbs was munching a huge crust of bread and lard, while the others, who had had no tea, looked enviously on. Claydabber Dick came slouching up from the darkness towards us. He saw the lad's crust and broke out, "Gie's a bit, Freddy, on'y a bit; just a little teeny bit. I've had nothin' sin soup time."

In reply Freddy gave him the whole. He began wolfishly devouring it; then, on a sudden thought, he broke a piece off. "It's for Katie," he said.

That touched us all. But we had no suppers to expect, so could not share them. And in hopeless silence we watched him pass into the darkness with the crust in his hand.

Next day, Dick was missing. Later on came news that he had been seen tramping to Birmingham with the intention of joining the Navy.

Two nights later we were in the same place at about the same time when Katie came up towards us. She saw us under the lamp, but turned aside her head, and for the first time passed us without a word or even a smile. She walked up into the street while we stared after her.

"I don't believe she's had anything t' eat," said Stubbs.

No one spoke.

Within an hour she came back. A young well-dressed man was on her, arm. He was smoking a cigar, an almost unknown luxury in Tumblefold. But as they passed under the lamp I saw that the girl's face was white and her beautiful eyes were stern and desolate. They went into the house together.

"She's got a fresh chap," said one; "ain't he a toff? But what'll Tommy Turner say when he comes over on furlough?"

We remained there for an hour or two, but that door opened not again.

Next night at the same hour she came out and returned soon after with another young man even better dressed than the other. He, too, stayed a long time. Next day Katie came through the Fold wearing a new dress, a new hat, and even new boots. At night she had yet another escort. Then we guessed the truth. She was selling her body to feed her helpless mother and workless father. The elders had guessed it before, and the question had been bandied carelessly about, "Heard the latest?   Irish Katie's on the streets."

At first the disgrace of it weighed on her, and she kept indoors till night.   When she appeared she spoke to none, but walked through with the same white face and stern set eyes we had seen that other night.

But at last she became hardened to it, and joined in with the neighbours, who, knowing the cause, treated her fall as mercifully as they hoped their God would.   For they had a God, most of them, though He seemed to have disowned them.

She was no longer our Katie.   Her youth, her merry, careless laugh, and her store of girlish fun were gone.   She sang no more songs.   Her laugh grew hard and sneering, as did her eyes.   She had the look of one who had learned the truth, the absolute truth, of something which all her life she had fiercely refused to believe.

Suddenly her mother died.   And while no blinds were down, and the body was hidden away in a windowless room, Katie went out by day as well as by night in order to raise the money for the coffin and the grave.

They buried the mother.   The next night Katie went out again, and returned with the usual unknown escort. Her father was in the Spotted Dog, drinking and playing cards. He had been flush of money since Katie went on the streets.

A few minutes afterwards a soldier came striding down the Fold, and passed us quickly. As he went under the lamp we just saw his face. It was Tom Turner. He walked straight down to her door, and opened it as unceremoniously as he always did before he went soldiering.

"I wonder if he knows," said Stubbs; "won't there be a row if he don't? Let's go down quietly."

Three or four went down, quickly and stealthily. We had just gained the door when we heard a scream, the door opened suddenly, and the stranger, bleeding from a cut on his head, rushed hatless and coatless through the Fold.

Facing each other in the bare kitchen were Tom Turner and Katie. His eyes were fixed on her in hate and loathing. Her hands were lifted imploringly. But, oh, that sweet, white face, and the agony in her eyes!

"Don't," she cried, "don't go like that. Say only one word to me, Tom. *Do* forgive me. I was forced to it, God Almighty knows I was. Tom, say you forgive me. I don't want you to touch me, to look at me, to think of me ever again, but for God's sake, Tom, tell me that."

In her agony she had clutched his arm, but he shook her hand from him with a shudder, as though her touch had been contagion. He looked for a space that seemed an age at the white face withering under his eyes. Then he uttered one word, a word nameless here, struck her brutally across the face with the heavy end of his cane, and strode away into the night, leaving her lying silent and bleeding on the floor.

.   .   .   .   .

Next day the shutters were closed, and the house was empty. Never, never again was Katie seen in Tumblefold.

CHAPTER XX

JOHNNY YEUBREY'S GARDEN

I WAS Johnny Yeubrey, and I suppose I should have written as the title of this story, "My Garden." But somehow—perhaps because Tumblefold is so far away, and it is all so long ago—I can never convince myself that Johnny Yeubrey and I are one and the same; and when I look back I see a ricketty, pale-faced lad, whose thin limbs were mocked by his sack-like clothes, cut down from old suits of his uncle's. And as I think of him playing wearily between school hours, staring hungrily in shop windows on winter nights, or lying awake in the darkness, wondering, in terror that dogged him through his dreams, if it was true, as the neighbours mercilessly told him, that he was in a consumption and would never make a man of—I cannot help muttering in musing pity, "Poor old Johnny." Then I think with a smile of his garden, one of the few good things that he found on his lonely march to manhood. And though he has walked in many gardens since then, some almost Eden-like in beauty, not one has seemed so rare and pretty as the one which long ago he fashioned on the roof of an old fowl-pen, to the delight and wonder of all the children in Tumblefold.

To the children of the slums the lowliest child of the earth was something to be loved and fondled, and the moss which grew on some of the damp walls, and the lonely blades of grass which grew between the stones in out-of-the-way corners of the Fold, were held in strange reverence.

If some woman, in reckless generosity, bought a penny bunch of flowers on market day, she usually regretted it, for the children swarmed round her, crying, "Gi'e me a flower, please; only a little 'un," or begging just to smell them.

If a cart laden with clover went along Susbury Road, there was quickly a crowd of youngsters behind it, and those who could secure one or two clover tufts felt rich, for they had favours to grant, and could say "No" or "Yes" to the entreaty, "Let us smell yer flower."

With death they became early acquainted, and it had no particular terrors for them. But the flowers, that could not speak, or lie, or get drunk, or steal; the flowers, always pure, and sweet, and pretty—they could not understand why these should die. Many a child has gone along the gutter and the walls, scraping up all the loose soil it could find, to form a little heap, in the midst of which would be placed some treasured flower, perhaps a discarded rose from some respectable coat, which had been picked up in the street and joyfully brought home; and as the children gathered round, and saw the flower fall helplessly across the bit of earth, there was a sorrow in their eyes which the presence and shadow of death in their own homes had no power to bring. Again and again would they prop up the frail stem; nor would they have been surprised had the rootless thing blossomed before their eyes. There is something beautiful in a child's— even a slum child's—optimistic and unquestioning confidence in life and tacit contempt of death.

Johnny Yeubrey became very early one of these little slum gardeners, and with him the illusion lasted much longer than with the others. He had an uncle who lived somewhere in the country, and sent bunches of flowers sometimes, which were placed in the window, so that all who went by might see them. There was a box of musk in Yeubrey's window, too,

and this was the only green thing that grew
in Tumblefold.

Sometimes his mother allowed him to water
the musk, and the honour was so great that
he must needs share it with his chums; and
they took turns in pouring out, with many a
"Steady, y'r puttin' too much on."

A year or two later Johnny's big brother
told him there were insects on the musk, and
asked him to smoke a bit at a penny cigar,
which he produced. Johnny had only indulged in whiffs at a communal cigarette
before, but he didn't let on that he was not
used to smoking: so he commenced on the
penny cigar, but did not finish it. His brother
said it would kill the insects. It nearly killed
Johnny: but, of course, that has nothing to do
with the story of his garden.

Between Yeubrey's house and the next was
a narrow passage, about two feet wide, called
the "Gullet." Johnny's father, with a few
planks and other things, added to the two walls
a roof and back and front doors, making
thereby a pen in which he kept fowls.

It was fairly substantial in parts, and
Johnny and his chums used to enjoy getting
on the roof of this pen on summer nights and
telling tales or dreaming of what they would
do when they went to work.

There was a breath of the adventurous

about it, too.   They used a ladder to get to the top. It was minus two of the bottom staves, but they never bothered which end was uppermost. They usually stayed on the roof till dark, and forgot before they came down whether the staveless end was top or bottom.   Then on a point of honour they grew chivalrous, and it was "You goo down fust, Johnny; it's your roof, y' know, an' you always ought to goo fust."   And Johnny went; sometimes more expeditiously than he expected or relished.   It was only a low roof, six feet high at the front and four at the back, and the ladder was not really needed.   But it looked more imposing and adventurous, so they used it.

One night, early in spring, the five lads were sitting on the next roof, dangling their feet over the fowl pen.   Johnny was looking meditatively at one of the blades of grass that were growing in a spout just out of reach. Suddenly he exclaimed:

"*I* say, let's mek a garden."

"Weer?" said Ryder, sarcastically, "on the roof?"

"Ah!"* said Johnny, so promptly that Ryder's bottom jaw fell and his mouth opened in utter discomfiture, "well 'ave it on the roof o' the fowl pen, an' we'll grow pansies,

---

* South Staffordshire: "Yes."

an' roses, an' gillyflowers, an' minniernett—
eh, we *will* 'ave a garden."

Johnny was excited, and his sudden rush of
ideas forced the words out so rapidly that he
nearly toppled over the roof.

"But we've got no sile," said Potter,
dubiously.

"Don't matter," said Johnny, "I know a lane
weer there's plenty all in th' edges. Let's goo
an' get some now; we can get enough to-night
to cover the roof."

His enthusiasm was catching, and they
caught it. Saying nothing of their enterprise
to the others, away they went, with bags and
baskets, and came back laden and perspiring.

In the darkness they raised the ladder and
began carrying the soil up on a shovel, taking
turns. Johnny was on top, spreading out the
soil. Operations went on rapidly till Jones
missed his step when near the top and let go
the soil but not the shovel.

As the earth clattered into the darkness below, there was a terrific uproar and yells of:

"The roof's tumbled in an' berried us. Oh,
Mother!"

"I'm blinded, it's all gone in my eyes.
Murder!"

"Let's get out quick, I'm berried alive."

Then, as they heard the irrepressible chuckle
above, the wailing changed to threats, and:

"All right, Jones, yer did it on purpose, yer did."

"Wait till yer come down," yelled Potter, "yer fatheaded Pig. I'll knock yer bloomin' eye out."

"Who will?" retorted Jones, losing his temper at once.

"*I* will," said Potter, bellicosely; "come down the bloomin' ladder."

But a fight was not desirable, so Johnny interfered and smoothed things over. There were no more accidents till the soil was all carried up, when the five chums mounted the ladder to examine the garden, which occupied but a little space as yet.

"We'll 'ave to fetch some more to-morrow," said Johnny; "come on." So they went down safely, with the exception of Ryder, who put his foot on a plank in the roof that wasn't there, and knocked the old cock off his perch. And the row those fowls made was so great that the neighbours came out and suggested "burglars"; what time the five little boys cowered in the darkness against the wall and pretended they were not a bit frightened by the acrimonious cackling and the wings that were flapping about them.

The next night they fetched more soil, and still there was not enough. They intended putting a thickness of two feet on the roof; but when, after nightly journeys for a fortnight, they saw that their labours had only covered the roof to the depth of several inches, they began to have compunction and saw the iniquity of the deeds they were doing in carrying away so much soil without the knowledge of the owners.

"It's stealin', that's wot it is," said Potter to Johnny; " 'ow would you like it to be done to your garden?"

Johnny could not answer; so they began discussing what they should have in the garden. The general idea was flowers—Jones did suggest "taters," and nearly fell off the roof at the derisive chorus.

"*Taters in a garden!* Oh, you bloomin' Fathead."

Ryder was inclined to leave the soil there and wait and see what grew.

"Ger away," said Johnny, in his most superior manner, "y'll 'ave to sow seeds, else nothin' 'll come up. That's wot my uncle sez, an' 'e's got a garden, ain't 'e?"

But Ryder persisted: "I'm talkin' about great big fields, weer there's daisies, and bluebells, an' buttercups, an' all of them. An' I know them seeds ain't sowed—they just come up, an' if y' leave this alone y' don't know what might come up—p'raps a big oak tree."

"I shouldn't let it grow," said Johnny, in

sudden solicitude for his father's fowl pen. "W'y, the roots 'ud pull the walls down in a month. No, I'm goin' to sow some seed, I am."

"Well, I ain't fetchin' any more sile," said Ryder, discontentedly.

Johnny waxed angry.

"Look 'ere, this is our fowl pen, ain't it?"

"I know it is," said Ryder.

"An' ain't this our Gullet; couldn't I turn yer all out now, if I wanted to?"

This alarmed the other three, who looked indignantly at Ryder.

"An' ain't this my garden?" queried Johnny, loftily.

"We 'elped yer to carry the sile."

"Well, wot if yo' did? I didn't ax yer to, did I? Think I couldn't a done it meself?"

"I know weer they sell flower seeds in penny packets," said Ryder.

"Do yer?" said Johnny, in joy at this tacit surrender; "I've got tuppence; let's goo an' buy some."

So the five lads went away to the seedsman, who was considerably surprised by his customers, but, having still a bit of the boy left in him, went to great pains to convince them that they could not buy all the seeds in his shop for twopence; and, besides, even if they could, it would hardly do to sow roses, and mignonette, and pansies, and pinks, and snow-drops all at the same time; which was a dis-appointment, for they had an idea that they had only to put the seeds in the ground, and then sit on the next roof and watch the flowers come up.

So he gave them mignonette and nasturtium seeds, one or two little green plants from his counter, and something which he said was a sunflower, and if they looked after it, it would grow as high as a man, and would have a flower "as big round as a plate." Then, with an amused smile, he watched them go away, talking excitedly.

They sowed the seeds; gave the sunflower the place of honour on the highest end of the roof, and then, night after night, for a week or two, they sat on the adjoining roof, looking down into the garden, which refused to bloom into beauty all at once. They knew where the seeds were placed, and at times the temp-tation was great to remove the earth and see how they were getting on. But it might have meant death to the garden, and curiosity had to wait.

Of course, the other children had heard of it, and were anxious to see the garden; but Johnny's father refused to let him take them in a body through his fowl pen, so they had to be content with seeing Johnny and his chums sitting on the roof. This caused bad feeling, and, acting on the sour grapes principle, the others ridiculed the garden and its gardeners night after night, and sometimes threw stones, with the intention of spoiling any flower that might be growing. This led to determined sorties from the roof garrison, and after one or two fights the stone-throwing ceased.

They had a lot of trouble with cats. That garden seemed to be a source of wonder to all the cats in Wolverhampton, and night after night they held open-air concerts thereon; and every morning Johnny mounted the ladder, ruefully regarding some trampled favourite. So they took to chivying every cat they could see, and for weeks the cats in Tumble-fold fled precipitately at sight of any one of the five gardeners.

But the spring wore on, and in spite of cats and envious chaff, and sarcastic enquiries from the neighbours of "What's the price o' taters, Johnny?" and "Likely to 'ave a good crop o' turnips this time?" the garden grew and flourished, and the delight of the lads was great as they sat on the roof and looked lovingly at their garden. The sunflower waxed tall, and soon was as high as the spout, while the nasturtiums growing against the walls, and the fragrance of the mignonette, effectively

silenced the scoffing of the others, for even
from the outside the taller plants could be seen,
and the sunflower was the admiration of all
who went by.

There was a small space in which no seeds
had been sown, just to please Ryder, and
curiosity was great as to what would come up;
and, strangely enough, this was the first part
of the garden to bring up anything. Ryder
was jubilant, and Johnny began to wish he
had left a bigger space untouched. Whatever
it was it grew apace—so fast that in a couple
of months it had sprawled across the narrow
part of the garden, and had crowded out of
existence a big bed of six pansies. There
were many conjectures as to what it might be.
Freddy Stubbs suggested "Peanuts," and was
laughed at. "Peanuts grow on trees as big
as a 'ouse," said Jones. Johnny's father said
it was a "Jeroosalum archioke," which seemed
plausible enough, as they had never seen one.
His uncle, who came to see it, smiled, and said,
"Let it grow, Johnny, it's all right": which
seemed to confirm the father's statement, and
the boys bragged greatly about the "Jeroosalum archioke" which had sprung up without
any seed.

But just as wickedness found its way into
the Garden of Eden, so did it enter the smaller
Eden in Tumblefold. There was one of the

"roughs," Billy Churm by name, who was offended by constant refusals to let him see the garden, and who was always making obnoxious remarks concerning it in the hearing of the gardeners.

Jones fought him one night and beat him, which intensified the ill-feeling. A night or two later Billy, with a gang of his sympathisers, stood outside and cast rude remarks and stones at the property owners on the roof. Of course they came down, and there were several fights; but the gang still remained; and just as it was getting dark, Billy clambered over the shoulders of two confederates on to the garden, to the great wrath of the astonished gardeners.

"Hey, you hook it," yelled Johny. "This is our garden; ye've no business 'ere. Fetch a bobby, somebody."

"D'y 'ear," yelled Potter, "ger off; this is our garden."

"No, it ain't," shouted back Billy, with a derisive grin; *"part on it's mine."*

"W-W-Wot yer mean," said Johnny, utterly astonished.

"Why," said Billy, still grinning, "I want my taters"—pointing to the "Jeroosalum archioke"—*them's taters, them is.* I climbed up one night after you'd gone down and put a tater in; *an' them taters is mine."*

Without another word, hardly caring whether they smashed the plants or not, the gardeners fell on him and there was a fight, in which Billy was mauled. They didn't stay long on the roof. They struggled, of course, to the weakest part of it, and they all went through, followed by tree-pots, planks, and tiles, and what seemed to be millions of tons of soil. What with the crash of their fall, their cries in fighting, and the noise of the fowls they had unroosted in mid-air, there was as pretty a Babel as could be desired or heard.

They did not release the invader, but pounded him on the floor; and when Johnny's mother and father and all the family wrathfully went to the rescue, Billy was in a very bad state.

He went for his "taters," so he said; but the gardeners gave him "beans" instead, and of them he had quite a surfeit.

But there were no more evening pleasures on the roof. Johnny was forbidden to ever climb the roof again, and had to give way. The loss was not so great as it might have been, for there was not much left of that roof. The sunflower remained, lonely but glorious, and they stood outside and watched the great flower for many a night; but it died down in its course, and a few months later the old building next door was pulled down, and the

Gullet, the fowl pen, and the garden that used to be on the top thereof, became things of the past.

And that was the end of Johnny Yeubrey's Garden.

But Johnny has not forgotten it.

CHAPTER XXI

THE QUARREL

HOW it came about would be a hard thing to say. There were various plausible reasons put forward by each at the time, but very hazy and weak they were. We had often been very near fighting at times, but even then had kept from quarrelling. The only theory I can think of, even now, is that several years of unbroken comradeship had become somewhat monotonous. Even sweetness cloys, they say. So one day, after a queer, sultry atmosphere had hung over us for a week, we seized the opportunity, and fell out.

We were trotting down to school, when Potter rebuked Jones sharply for some error in speech. This was nothing unusual, but Jones turned very red, and retorted:

"Who are you talking to? You know a lot too much, you do."

Potter stared, caught the offensive tone, and promptly ignored him. This, of course, could not long go on. Ryder looked round, then at me, and whispered: "I say, Johnny, old Potter was too sharp on Jones, wasn't he?"

I was just about making that same remark to Ryder, but of course I could not after he had made it. So, having caught the infection, I replied, "Too sharp? No. Jones is too cheeky."

Ryder looked up, angrily. He had caught it badly. "Too cheeky, eh?" he said, with a forced sneer; "well, *I'm* one with him, anyhow."

I turned round, and spoke to Potter. We went on, with Freddy in the middle, looking rather astonished. Potter and I talked to him, and ignored the other two; they in turn did the same. If we had anything to say interesting to them, we said it loudly to Freddy. They followed suit.

It was indeed a complicated quarrel. Freddy tried artfully and hard to reconcile the two factions, but was only snubbed for his pains. We were silent in school, and the teacher stared. We were evidently not on speaking terms.

The difficulty was—what were we to do with Freddy? It was clearly unfair to him to have a quarrel in which he could not participate. Besides, if he could be won over to either side it meant three against two, and something for the three to crow over.

Potter and I decided to get at him that same night. We found him with Jones and Ryder. On seeing us they walked away without speaking. We stared at them with the greatest unconcern.

"Look here, Freddy," said Potter, "you've got to come on our side. We shan't speak to them again."

"Why?" asked Freddy, blankly.

"Why?" said Potter, growing angry, as he always did when cornered; "because we shan't, that's why."

Freddy was obstinate. He had no idea what the quarrel was about, and we could not tell him. And, as his one reply to our remarks was, "What's the matter? What's it all about?" we left him in disgust.

He refused to take sides. For the next few days he was trotting backwards and forwards between us, and vainly trying to mend the breach. It was impossible, he was told, with becoming dignity. Each side told him all kinds of stories, and made groundless insinuations concerning the others. Both alike were to him incredible and mean, and, besides, were wicked. Freddy was a lad who never said ill of another, whether absent or present, and rebuked it in others.

At last his efforts succeeded so far that each side informed him casually that if the other two would abase themselves by speaking first, all might be well. Which message was duly delivered, and the reply from both sides was, "You tell 'em we can do without 'em. We'll never, never speak to 'em again." And the unfortunate mediator went on the trot once more.

We were all exceedingly miserable, but refused to own it. Play was out of the question. Our games had for months been adapted to a combination of five, and two could not play them. So we glared at each other or talked fussily to Stubbs. We tried to look unconcerned and as if we would not welcome with joy the first approaches from the other side.

The roughs got wind of it, and were jubilant on seeing the friendship of years at an end. They did their best to widen the breach, carried tales from one side to the other of real or imaginary insults and allegations, listened to the vain threats in reply, and promptly carried them back.

One night Potter and ·I stood under our

window. Jones and Ryder sauntered up and stood against the wall about a yard away from us. Stubbs came and faced the two couples silently.

"I'll tell you what," said Potter to me, just loud enough for them to hear; "I'll tell you a story."

That was a keen thrust. They winced, looked eager, but never moved.

"Yes, do," said Stubbs, looking at them in mute entreaty.

They moved a little farther away.

Potter looked at me and went on, "It's about——"

"Rats!" said Ryder to Jones, loudly, but without looking at us.

I looked at Stubbs. We were all under our window. "Freddy Stubbs," said I, "if some cheeky kids would move on to their own buildin', there wouldn't be such a smell round here."

Potter sniffed. "It's awful," he said, spitting. "Never smelt such a stink before. Ugh! it's beastly. Must be his feet."

Ryder turned very red. Jones said to Stubbs, "We shall stand under whose winder we like, without askin' anybody's leave, and if you know any Fat-headed Monkey what wants to fight, you put him on to me, will yer?"

"What wants to fight," said Potter, pityingly, to Stubbs. "Strewth, what grammar!"

"What wants to fight," repeated Jones, emphatically, to Stubbs, "and if he's frightened, I'll fight him with one hand, kneelin' down."

Freddy stood in the middle, facing the four, and looking unutterably miserable. He expected a fight every minute.

"Cuckoo!" said I.

"Cock-a-doodle-doo!" crowed Potter, mockingly.

"Rats!" said Ryder, savagely.

"Rats," repeated Potter, to Freddy. "I know why he says it. His father catches 'em."

"Don't, Potter," implored Freddy; "you shouldn't say such things. You know you shouldn't."

Ryder was not put out, and remarked loudly, "I'd sooner catch rats than fleas. Ugh-h-h!" with a shiver, "there's one on me now. I know where it came from."

Jones had a word now; with Freddy, of course. "My father goes to the Spotted Dog, but he always wipes his chalk off."

This delicate allusion irritated Potter.

"Ugh! what a smell," he said, holding his nose; "I wish they'd shift."

This was equally irritating to Jones and Ryder. For nearly an hour we carried on the same foolish game, then in sheer disgust all five went indoors. Freddy was much relieved. He had quite expected a fight.

The next day was just the same. Our anger was heightened by our knowledge all the time that we were ridiculous young fools. There was no reason for the quarrel, there was no reason why we should not follow our own inclinations and join hands again. Freddy, dearer to all than ever, argued and entreated, but each pair was stubborn, and firmly resolved never to speak to the others again. Never, never again.

Two nights later the fight came off. It was inevitable from the beginning. The roughs saw their opportunity, and were bent on having a fight. Such a thing had never happened before, and to see four of the five chums fighting was a luxury that might come only once in a lifetime.

All day they had been carrying threats from one side to the other, appealing to the vanity and coarser nature of each with such remarks as: "I say, Jones, you ain't gwine ter stand that, are you?"

"If I was you, Potter, I'd kick him, I would."

By the time it was dusk we were all in a murderous mood. Freddy had given up all hope of mending matters, and hung round miserably.

Just after tea the two factions met in a retired passage. Urged on by the excited outsiders, the two couples stood facing each other, hands in pockets, and staring defiantly. The crowd closed round, and jostled them together.

"Who are yer shovin'?" said Jones, angrily.

"Who are you shoving?" inquired Potter, with the accent on the "g."

"Shevving!" laughed Jones, mimicking Potter's voice and accent, "who am I shevving? I'm a shevving you."

He turned to the crowd, who laughed and egged the pair on.

Potter was quite cool, and remarked: "Next time you shove me fetch your best things out of pawn, and do it with clean hands."

The crowd howled with delight. Jones went white as he saw Potter brush some imaginary dirt from his clothes. He went up to him, threateningly.

"Don't you touch me," said Potter, apprehensively. "I might catch something."

"Who are you as you shouldn't be touched?" inquired Jones.

"Don't touch me again."

"I will touch him."

"Well, touch him, that's all."

"D'yer think I dursent?"

"No, you dursent."

"What about that, then?" "That" was a gentle tap with two fingers. "I have touched him, see?"

"Touch him to hurt him," said Potter, calmly.

"I will."

"Well, do it."

Jones had no option. The crowd pushed him, and he pushed Potter rather roughly. Potter struck him. That settled it.

"*Oh!*" said Jones, as if he had not suspected it before, "you want to fight, do yer? Come on!"

"Come on!"

Much the same dialogue had passed between Ryder and myself. We devoutly wished ourselves out of it, but the roughs were bantering and bullying behind, and there was no escape. Coats were taken off, and piled on Freddy, sleeves were turned up, and without any more ado we spat on our hands and began fighting.

As far as Ryder and I were concerned, the fight was a fraud. We ducked our heads, charged, and resolutely struck the air and each other's back for five minutes; then we stood up, panting and perspiring.

"Have ye had enough?" said I.

"Yes, have you?"

"I have!"

We shook hands, glad it was no worse.

With the other two it was different. Potter's cool sarcasm had maddened the short-tempered Jones, and both being about the same size, the fight was a long one. Potter's nose was bleeding, and Jones had a black eye. As soon as our fight ended, Freddy came up in terror. "They'll be killed," he said. "Let's stop 'em. Come on."

He rushed, coats and all, between them, and was promptly punched. The coats, however, protected him. The roughs yelled, "Come out o' that."

The biggest of them, who had taken Claydabber's place as leader, was an arrant coward. Being twice as big as Freddy, he rushed in to fight him. He struck at him, but missed.

At that moment the other two were striking off over Freddy's head. Jones saw the coward's blow, and in an instant the old clannish feeling came back. He received unresistingly a blow from Potter, who had not seen it, then went for the bully, who had struck again at Stubbs and hurt him. There was a short, fierce fight, which Jones won easily. Then he came back to Potter, with a queer light in his eyes. "Shall we finish it?" he asked, hesitatingly. It was plain he did not want to finish it.

Potter could easily win now, but he was prompt and generous. "No! I won't fight you any more. I'll stand for you to lick me first."

Jones' sound eye beamed, while the damaged one tried to do so, and failed. "Shake hands, ol' chap, we're chums again."

We all shook, just as a policeman's advent scattered the disappointed crowd. A few minutes later we were in Jones' backyard, washing faces, and chatting as volubly as ever.

Jones stroked his eye. "Is it very black?" he asked.

"Not very," said Potter; "it'll be all right in two days. How's my face?"

Jones grinned. "The skin's all off yer nose."

Freddy could hardly contain himself. At last he broke out: "Now it's all over, and we're chums again, p'r'aps you'll tell me what it was all about."

Ryder looked at me, Jones looked at Potter. Finally we all looked hopelessly at Freddy. Nobody knew.

"I'll tell you what," said Potter, seriously, after a long pause, "I think we've all been fools."

This was emphatically agreed to by all, including Freddy, who was not included.

And that was the only conclusion we ever came to in the matter.

CHAPTER XXII

OF course, we all went to the same Sunday school, usually morning and afternoon. This was a token of our respectability, and in its way was a great infliction.

We had to go with clean faces, clean hands, and boots; while the roughs, those of them who went at all, attended a Sunday night school where the lessons and teachers were adapted to them. They went just as they were; and when there, pleased themselves whether they played tattoo on the forms, or listened to the teachers. This was a freedom we envied.

Morning school was dull and dry, but we attended regularly till Potter discovered that the School Board man never mentioned Sundays. So we stopped away on Sunday mornings, and went long walks instead.

Sunday afternoon was different. The school was fuller, and the lessons more interesting.

There was a different staff of teachers, too, who were popular for the reason that they knew a little of boy nature, and taught accordingly. But, alas, for their innocence, and, one must say it, too often ignorance. The street boy is quick-sighted, and swift at conclusions.

The afternoon was spent in reading a chapter from the Bible, each lad reading a verse in turn, and the teacher illustrating by remarks and suggestions the lesson to be learned. Of course, every chapter had its lesson. But there were often the objectionable passages cropping up, and the blushing teacher would hurriedly direct us to pass over the passage—pretending not to notice the significant and knowing smile which passed round the class. We always knew when these passages were coming, and studied them beforehand. And it is unquestionable that the degrading suggestiveness of the evil placed in our hands often nullified the simple moral truths which were taught.

But Sunday school had its advantages. Once every year, usually on August bank holiday, came the school treat, when the children were taken from the town to some pleasant haunt, and there revelled in the fresh air and green grass.

Every year, for about a month before the

event, the school became visibly bigger, and on the Sunday when the treat tickets were given out it was overcrowded. This was due to the sudden awakening to piety of dozens of children, who had discovered that their spiritual natures needed cultivation. So after an absence of months they came to Sunday school, and attended earnestly to the teachers.

It was rather strange that these revivals should always happen just before the treat, and the scholars who attended all the year round imputed very mean motives to them. Sometimes it was shouted from class to class: "Yah, yer snooger, you've only come to get a ticket for the tea-party."

The newcomers bore this with great fortitude, while the teachers said "Hush, hush," and tried to look as if they did not believe that half the lads were tea-craving, bun-worshipping hypocrites.

One year a change was made in the programme. It was decided to have a huge trip by boat along the canal to Brewood, an old village about nine miles from Wolverhampton. Instead of limiting it to our school, the Sunday night school was included, and also an adult class, composed largely of elderly married females.

We were delighted. Boating, even on the canal, was a luxury, and the prospect of gliding over the water for nine miles through green fields almost turned our heads.

Days went by, and we looked out eagerly every morning to see if it rained or threatened rain. The morning came at last, and after much brushing of hair, scrubbing of faces, and polishing of boots, we five ran to the schools. Here the usual procession was formed by perspiring teachers, and the many-coloured flags and banners, so dear to children, were given out. We were eager for the post of standard-bearers, Stubbs excepting. Wherefore, they gave him one of the heaviest, and ignored us.

Headed by our school drum-and-fife band we marched down Susbury Road till we came to the canal, where the boats (coal boats emptied for the occasion) were waiting. To us they were more wonderful than the *Great Eastern,* and the shrieks of fear as the boats were boarded were ear-splitting.

A great rush was made for the boat which held the band. The adult class, being privileged by age, had boarded it first, and sternly admonished the juveniles to be quiet, and not to rock the boat.

Many of the younger ones had never even seen a canal before, and the sight of the long, dirty creep of water, with green fields dotted with trees and cows and sheep on each side, had the strangest effects. Some cried, many danced and yelled and pushed one another about on the towing path; while others, who had been before, looked on patronisingly, and informed the awe-stricken juniors that it would be just the same all along the way! No houses, no smoke, no factories, no stacks, and no dirty gutters—whatever could it all mean?

The Vicar, his curate, and the teachers had a task which made them sweat under the hot morning sun. But every child was stowed somehow in the boats. The signal was given, the clergymen boarded our boat, the band struck up, and we started to the tune:

"Sailing, sailing, over the bounding main."

To be sure there were no sails to be seen, and the bony horses tugging along on the towing path were somewhat prosaic. But we did not mind. We were out for the day, and a great day it was.

The elderly females, being constitutionally afraid of water, kept in the middle of the boat, cajoled the unfortunate vicar into their midst, and kept him there. When the boat lurched, they shrieked.

Some of the children leaned over the side, and watched the panorama of green fields and trees in silent joy. Many crowded round the band, and those important young men, out of sheer vanity, played till their lips were sore. Then a chubby little curate came, and told us funny stories, sang songs, and pointed out everything in the fields we passed. The elderly ladies grew jealous, and forcibly tore him away, asserting that our noise would make his poor, dear head ache.

This caused bad blood, and without any hesitation we sat on the edge of the boat and rocked it. Then began open warfare. The more they shrieked, the more we rocked. What business had they in our boat, spoiling the fun? The curate enjoyed it and roared. The vicar, of course, could not laugh, and sat still.

Presently the elderly ladies waxed furious, and used threats. There were now about thirty smiling boys sitting on each side. We rocked the boat.

"You impudent wretches," shrieked a florid lady of about eighteen stone, flourishing a huge gingham, "you've shook my inside up, you have."

There was a lurch, and she collapsed with a gasp on the lap of the unfortunate vicar.

"Really," he said, as he tried and failed to encompass her with his arms, and let her slip to the floor, "really, boys—er— really——" Then, as the result of a similar lurch, he sat by her side on the floor. A bevy of frantic females rushed towards us, but a huge lurch sent them reeling into each other, and after loud, very loud, words they retired, and molested us no more.

It was a day of days. Even the birds seemed too happy or too lazy to sing, and we tried to make amends for them as we leaned over the side watching the green fields and waving corn. Country yokels came and stared at the white-faced town children, grinning in response to our facetious comments.

Sometimes the boat went so near to the hedges that we could pluck the foxgloves and wild flowers on the banks, and sometimes a dead creature floating on the waters would be an object of juvenile pity. Then there was the excitement of passing the locks, and every now and then the query, "What'll we do if the ship sinks?" It was a real three-decker to us—none of your common canal-boats.

A few miles out we came on a party of town youths bathing, as innocent of clothing as Adam was at first. There was great excitement on board. The girls looked at each other, and furtively at the grinning youths in the water. The lads shouted remonstrances, while the young lady teachers blushed and counted the planks in the floor of the boat. But the elderly persons—words could not measure their indignation. They rushed to the side of the boat, and we made for the other side by way of ballast. They shouted, shrieked, and brandished umbrellas. "You wretches! you wicked wretches! Aren't you ashamed—exposin' yourselves on a day like this before decent, respectable people and innocent children. Hoo!"

The vicar smiled; the curate laughed immoderately. We rocked the boat; they shrieked, turned their terrified heads round, and saw that they were trapped. So they clung desperately to the side, said their prayers and raved at us in a breath, as we rocked the boat assiduously for at least ten minutes. When we had laughed so long that we had no strength left for rocking, we desisted, and they crawled to the middle of the boat in a state of mental and physical collapse. It was indeed an exciting passage, and fast too, for we ran the nine miles in three hours, less five minutes, and bragged about it for weeks.

After the trouble of embarking, getting out was a small matter, and soon the children, two hundred odd, were playing and rolling about in a large, undulating meadow covered with buttercups and daisies. The bigger ones adventurously went on voyages of discovery along lanes or into the village. We five kept together, but, like the others, gave vent to our feelings.

We were free. We were poor no longer. Yea, we were exceedingly rich. For one whole day we had inherited the earth, with the trees and the flowers and the light and fragrance of the grass and the sky.

We pushed each other over, we stood on our heads in the grass and turned somersaults and cartwheels till we were breathless. Then we climbed to the top of a steep little slope, and rolled from top to bottom so many times that Stubbs grew light-headed and stopped half-way. He was buried forthwith under an avalanche composed of Potter, Yeubrey, Ryder, and Jones. The whole laughing, yelling heap rolled down and over a miniature precipice, and altogether, good comrades as we were, made a clear drop of several feet into a bed of nettles.

This, with the shaking, cooled our blood, and we sat up ruefully looking at each other and comparing bumps and contusions.

We decided to have an interval, so climbed the hill again, and lay in the deep grass looking up at the sky and the trees. We talked quietly among ourselves, as usual; serenely happy, we could not help thinking of the morrow, and the day after the morrow, when we should be dwindling in Tumblefold. We yearned for a tea-party to come every day. It was our last year at school. We were just beginning to realise what we were losing, and what leaving school meant. And though we knew it not then, it was the very last holiday we five would spend together.

We lay listening drowsily to the shrieks and laughter of the others as they played in the field, or in and out among the trees. At last the welcome bell rang, and amid indescribable uproar the children were seated in dozens on the grass, while in an improvised canteen all was heat and work. Then the teachers and helps took their places, and tea, buns, cake, and bread and butter were soon in circulation. The instructions were, "Eat all, and pocket none."

The first part was obeyed, the latter was in many cases calmly ignored. There were few who had not left smaller children at home, and the tribal instinct was strong.

Ryder was happy, and beamed round benignly on us as he proceeded in his own words to "tuck it in." He afterwards confessed to the eating and drinking of six currant buns, four slices of bread and butter with jam, seven slices of cake, assorted, and nine cups of tea. After this he lay down, with a look of supreme self-satisfaction on his features.

Tea being ended, and all appetites satisfied, the games were restarted, but with less vigour. The teachers and elders, meanwhile, were enjoying the rewards of merit at a table artistically laid out near the tent. There were brisk flirtations and many expressive glances as they passed round the eatables. It is astonishing what worlds of meaning a young man can put into the simple sentence, "Will you please pass the sugar, miss?" And what queer feelings may be caused by the accidental meeting of two hands round a cream-jug!

But there is an end to all good things. The games were ended, the last race was run, and the last forfeit paid. With lessened noise, being tired, the children were marched to the towing-path, where the boats were waiting.

The elderly females were there before us. They were bent on boarding the boat which held the band. The juvenile bandsmen, and with them the bigger lads, were resolved that they should not. So they waited, and we waited, till all the boats were filled but one. Then, being compelled to go on board, we did so savagely. The elderly females followed us with a triumphant laugh; a laugh they regretted. The vicar was in the front boat, and the curate safe in our midst.

The band struck up, and with loud cheers for everybody and everything we started homewards.

It was plain from the first that there would be trouble in our boat. The lads were sitting in a row on each side, waiting for the signal.

The band began "Weel may the keel row." At the same time the boat began to rock. The ladies shrieked, and implored the curate to order them to desist. He replied that he positively could not, as he was overpowered by numbers. We meant paying off the morning's score, and rocked and lurched to larboard and starboard till the boat nearly capsized, while the elderly annoyances alternately threatened and cried, as they lurched into all kinds of ridiculous attitudes. As for the curate, he laughed till he burst his collar, and then laughed louder than ever.

The band maliciously began to play "The Dead March," and the boat moved with befitting slowness. The rocking continued, and we became so foolhardy that several times we nearly went over. But the names we were called by the elderly persons, and their devout prayers to set foot once again on dry land, were rich indeed, and added zest to the rocking torment, which went on till we were about half-way home.

Then, frightened by our noise and the demoniac uproar of the band, the horse towing our boat took a sudden jump, snapped the rope and bolted, leaving us helpless in mid-ocean.

There was an outcry, then. The curate

looked serious, the girls screamed, and the elderly persons poured out hysterical reproaches, and prayed spasmodically. We ran into a hedge, and as the boat recoiled, then went in again with a thud, we began to feel queer. What should we do if it sank?

We turned to the curate. He was smiling, and we felt braver. The other boats had gone on, and were now out of sight. The boatman was swearing on the towing-path. After much noise and trouble we managed to swing him the broken rope, and the runaway horse being brought up at the same time, the rope was spliced and we proceeded.

There was no more rocking. We were a little frightened; besides, we were nearing home. It was growing dark. The boat moved slowly and quietly through the shadows, and a strange silence enshrouded us all. Without knowing why, we talked in whispers. Then a girl began to sing, and gradually old and young joined in:

"Light in the darkness, sailor, day is at hand,
  See o'er the foaming billows fair haven's land.
  Drear was the voyage, sailor, now almost o'er,
  Safe within the lifeboat, sailor, pull for the shore!"

The words were not without a suspicion of bathos, but the tune, like most of Moody and

Sankey's melodies, was popular with us; and the religious feeling roused by the sombre shadows and the memories of the day's enjoyment, ended now and forever, was plainly visible on the hushed faces of the children.

It grew quite dark. We felt the boat just moving, we heard the dull swish as it brushed through projecting weeds and tree branches. We five were huddled together, as was our custom when tired. We came to the last mile, the prettiest part of the ride. For the whole distance, alongside the canal, was a rich man's estate, and a wonderful row of beeches stretched along the water's edge. The moon was up, and as we stared through the trees we saw a glory never to be forgotten. No one spoke or stirred. We five were feeling half-miserable, half-rebellious. To-day was ended —what of the morrow? Not for a whole year, may be never again, would we know a day like this. It seemed hardly fair in our sight.

We saw the lights on the last bridge, and heard the distant cries of the disembarked children. Someone began again:

"Light in the darkness, sailor, day is at hand."

"I wonder if it's true," said Ryder, "it don't seem like it to me."

He had echoed our thought, and we said

nothing. But Freddy, who had been looking fixedly overhead for the last mile, turned round, and said, in a tone he had never used before: "Look at the moon through the trees."

We looked up quickly. Then we joined in the hymn, and were almost contented as the last lines floated over the water, and the crowd on the bridge joined in.

"Bright gleams the morning, sailor, uplift the eye,
Clouds and darkness disappearing, glory is nigh."

And so we reached Wolverhampton. Quietly and thoughtfully we five went home. It may have been that the darkness, the beauty of the trees and the moonlight, and the sweet odours of the green fields and hedgerows, all combined with the mournful strength of the hymns to influence the emotional and sensitive minds of the children, and aroused to strange intensity that religious instinct which lies so deep in the heart of childhood.

It may have been merely so. Yet that home-coming had a great influence on the after-life of five lads in that gathering.

There is one of them to whom life has brought few pleasant paths and few acceptable lessons, who stands outside all orders and creeds, a sceptic and an image-breaker. And there are times when he, even he, lonely yet defiant in his isolation, longs with unexplainable desire for the faintest touch of the unquestioning faith he felt as he stared through the trees at the moonlight, one vanished summer night in the long, long ago.

CHAPTER XXIII

STUBBS

I SOMETIMES wonder what kind of men we four would have made had we never known Freddy Stubbs. He was so different from each of us, yet from the first he was the strongest of the links that held us together. He reconciled our differences, and smoothed our angularities. His weakness was his strength, and ours.

Till he came we were as rough as the rest, albeit a little more respectable. Our tendencies were by no means higher than our natures, and our moods were no lighter for our environment. Our motives were not of the purest, nor were our tongues of the cleanest. We were learning to use ourselves to our lot; to think that just as those around us drudged and drank, and between whiles, begat children, so, inevitably, should we in our turn drudge, drink, and beget children. It had no terror for us from the first, and it was beginning to have no shame. We were learning to lie, to slouch, to use foul words, and to harbour fouler thoughts.

When Freddy came he brought with him a clean heart and a clean atmosphere. He had been born and reared in the country,, and always in his eyes was an indescribable look suggesting flowers and sweetness. His mother was a refined, quiet woman, and though her coddling had weakened him physically, her influence had made his moral nature bright and strong. His was one of those white, quiet young faces which have always an unworldly suggestiveness about them, and often the light prophetic of early decay.

He came among us like a sunbeam into a dark room, and when he left us the light remained on our faces.

He had a fixed moral code. It was wicked to tell lies, to use foul words, to hate another, or take a mean advantage of any one weaker or duller than one's self. It was good to be plain and straightforward, to have clean words and right meanings, and to love everybody and everything. His religious nature was very strong. He always spoke of God in a whisper.

We laughed at him at first. We plagued him for his girlish ideas and ways, and tried to initiate him into our more manly courses. We tried, and failed. We told daring lies just to laugh at his rebuke. We used to steal marbles, chase smaller boys, pull the hair of any girl we met, and shout after cripples or old people, just to torment him. Once we threw stones at a sparrow, and brought it down. Freddy ran to where it fell, bruised and dying, and held it to him till it died. Then he cried, and went indoors. And, somehow, when he came out again, we could not face him.

He held us together. He was the one element needed to broaden and strengthen our lives. He developed and lit that side of our natures which Tumblefold had stunted and darkened. It happened at last that nothing mean or wrong could be said or done in his presence, and nothing ill was planned in his absence without an uneasy turn of the head lest he might be standing there.

His very weakness endeared him to us. It was something new from the first to have one who was so strangely dependent on our protection. We defended him on all occasions, and carried him even, when our walks tired him, with a boyish chivalry not altogether unworthy.

His mother and sisters were penniless, and had to work very hard for a bare living. They were ladies, all three, and were pleasant always, though they mixed but little with their neighbours. I am afraid they did not always get enough to eat, for they were thin and pale. But Freddy was always well looked after, and in hard times was ever ready to share his pieces with us.

He used to tell us stories of his early life; of his father, and a little sister who died; of the splendid garden, and the flowers, and the birds that came every morning for their breakfast; of the day when the home was sold up, and they went first to one place, and then to another, till at last they came to Wolverhampton and Tumblefold.

We often went into the house. His mother would show us the father's portrait, and the pictures, and a shelf full of books; sometimes, if we were good, letting us look through a portrait album, and telling us all about the portraits with that garrulous pride which is the one possession left to all who have seen better days.

Freddy was never strong. He might almost have been a disease barometer, for whatever epidemic was in the air it always found him out first. Sore throats in summer, and coughs and colds in the winter were unfailing visitors. His days and weeks in bed cut great gaps out of our playtime.

Once, after an illness, he joined us with a dark, thoughtful look on his face. He told us he had overheard the doctor whisper to his mother that she would have a very hard task to rear him.

"And I've been wondering," said Freddy, "when I was all by myself, if I should die, should I go to heaven."

We were sure of that.

"I don't know," said Freddy, "I've done a lot of wicked things. And—and—besides, I don't want to die now, and we've been so jolly, you know, we five together, and had such fun. Do you remember the tea-party last August, and coming back in the moonlight? I was wondering about it then, I don't know why, but I thought if next summer you go there again, and I—I aren't with you—I thought, you know, if I should be away, right away up there in the stars, ever so far up, p'raps I shall see you all, if you don't see me, and I shall be with you and we'll still be five jolly old chums—and then—and then——" he said, putting his hand to his forehead, "I get so tired, and it all goes dark, and I don't seem a bit frightened."

We tried to cheer him, but in vain. Every day he grew visibly thinner.

The winter began early that year, and trade grew slack. Freddy caught cold in the first snow, and was indoors for a week. Then he came to school, but his coughing was fearful to hear. He was unusually cheerful, however, and we hoped for the best, till one morning we called for him, and were told that he was ill again. At night he was still in bed.

Play was out of the question, and we gathered moodily under our window, talking about everything, but, by silent consent, never speaking of Freddy. A party of lads came by and stared. "Hello," said one, "there's one of 'em missin'. What's up? Who is it? Why, it's Freddy Chicken."

We savagely chased and punished the offender. But even as we came back Jones said gloomily, "We shouldn't have done it. Freddy wouldn't have liked it."

A week went by. Freddy was still in bed. "No better," was the answer to our queries morning, noon, and night. A few days later we were allowed to go and see him. He was thinner than ever, and flushed, and coughed all the time. But there was the same cheerful smile, and the same irresistible greeting.

Yes, he was getting better, the doctor said, and would soon be well now. After that we sat with him for an hour or two every night. He was getting better all the time, so the doctor said. But the cough was no better.

We talked of everything in our boyish way, and Freddy joined eagerly in it all. We planned out carefully what we would do when he got better; the games we would play (quiet ones, you know), and the walks we would take (not very long at first, you know); and on wet or very cold nights we would stay indoor and tell tales. Then, when he was quite strong again, we would go on just the old lines, and if we had a very big snow and a very hard frost we would build another Snow House, bigger even than the last, and with windows in it this time.

A month went by. Freddy was getting better, but was still in bed. One night we were told that he was just a little bit worse, and we must not see him. So the next night, and the next night. He had never been ill so long before. We had hitherto joined our pennies, and bought sweets and cakes for him. Now we were told that he must not have any more till he was better.

One night we were together under our window. The doctor had just come up from the darkness. We knew where he had been. As we stood there, Freddy's sister came to us. Had she been crying?

Yes, he was much better, and would soon be well now. He wanted us; would we go and sit with him?

We went quickly.

"Hush! come gently," said his mother, who stood waiting with a light at the head of the stairs. We crept on tiptoe to his room.

"How are we, chummies?" said Freddy; "I am glad you've come."

The voice was only a whisper. One look at his face was enough. Yes, he was getting better. He would soon be well now.

Ryder was the first to break down. He caught hold of the wasted hand, and buried his face in the bedclothes, sobbing. We were no stronger than Ryder.

"Don't, chummies," whispered Freddy, "don't cry. It hurts, you don't know how it hurts."

We watched him in silence. His eyes were staring up at the ceiling as if he saw something there that we could not see. He turned round suddenly.

"It's all right, chummies—I'm going to—heaven. I've seen it, you know, and—the gates are open. Yes—it's—all right. I went last—night. Dad was waiting—and—and—little Minnie. You—would be—surprised. She isn't a—bit older—and she laughed—roguish, you know—just—like—she used to. I told—them I—was—coming—and they were—glad. Yes—it's—all—right. But, I

say—chummies—you must come—not—yet—
you know—but—you—will come?"

We promised, one by one. He closed his
eyes. "I am—glad. Won't—we—have—a
—good—time!" Then, suddenly, in wistful
pain, "Shall you—miss me—very—much,
chummies?"

We were stronger now, and did not cry.
But not one might open his lips.

His eyes went to the ceiling again. His
lips began to move, but even whispering failed
him. But we knew that he was saying his
childish prayers. His mother motioned to us.
One by one we pressed the dear hand and
kissed the flushed cheek of our comrade; then
looked in the lad's loving eyes, and came away.
We turned as we reached the room door. His
eyes were watching us out.

Next morning, hoping against foreknowl-
edge, we went down to the house. The
shutter was closed, and the white blinds were
hung over the windows. Freddy was gone
home. We were only four now, on earth.
But he knew that still we were five.

＊   ＊   ＊   ＊   ＊

He was buried on Sunday. We put our
coppers together and bought a small wreath.

With it we went on Sunday morning to see him for the last time. All morning the children had been going up and down stairs. He looked beautiful in his coffin. His hands were folded, and on his pale face was the quiet, peaceful smile we knew so well. It was just the same dear face, and as we kissed him for the last time, we knew that all was well.

A few hours later the hearse came clattering down the passage, and the usual gaping crowd stood waiting to see the coffin. It came at last, his mother and sisters following. There were several wreaths, but at his head lay ours. The little door was closed, and slowly the hearse moved away. We four walked after it. We had no mourning, so wore none; that was in our hearts.

Down the long road it went, out of the town and through the suburbs till the cemetery was reached. We would have gone in, but being ragged and not respectable, were refused admittance. We stood looking through the gates till the coffin had passed from our sight, then, crying at the injustice which would not let us see the last of him we loved, we went home.

Freddy was gone, but his influence re-

mained. We were four, and yet were five.
Long after we had ceased to be affected by
the casual sight of some old plaything of his,
or some favourite haunt, we used to spend
hours in talking of the things we did and
thought in the days when we were five. If
any angry word, or low expression, or mean
impulse came to any one of us, it was checked,
sometimes by the words and always by the
thought, "What would Freddy say?"

That is a long time ago now. Times and
ways have altered since then. To me the years
have brought much of ill, and yet not a little
of good. Tumblefold is far away, a night-
mare, a dark abstraction.

Yet to me, as I write, and look for a moment
round my warm room, at her face who is
nearest and dearest and best-beloved to me, at
our little girl playing on the hearth, the books
piled on the shelves and in every corner, and
then go back to the past, there are few of our
belongings so dear as the little black-edged
card I have just taken from a box of old
mementoes. A little black-edged card, on
which are printed just these words:

In Affectionate Remembrance of
FREDERICK HENRY STUBBS,
Who died November 21st, 188—,
And was interred in Wolverhampton Cemetery,
November 25th, 188—
"For of such is the Kingdom of Heaven."

CHAPTER XXIV

THE EXAMINATION

WE had been preparing for it for weeks. Other examinations had been welcome and exciting breaks in the monotony of school life. We had year by year gone from class to class, and were now in the small but venerated class of lads who would leave school after this examination. Once, a few years before, we had been so pleased with the class we were then in, with the teacher, the lessons, and the intervals of secret fun, that we faced the examination determined not to pass.

We made the wildest replies to questions, and gave impossible solutions to the problems in arithmetic. Even Potter, whose pride was in his reading abilities, made such blunders and dropped so many aitches and final "g's" that the inspector angrily told him to sit down. We may have overdone it, however, for they passed us in a body to the next class.

This time it was serious. For months now we had been warned daily by our respective parents of what would happen if we failed in this examination. We had been at school long enough now, and it was time we turned out, and earned something towards our keep.

We had been looking forward to it for years, but now we were face to face with it the prospect was hardly so inviting. Our schooldays had been happier and brighter than we had known or thought, and our hearts were fain to go back and begin it all over again. There is a might-have-been even in a street lad's life.

It was the inevitable, and we faced it. We had been fettered, true, in the past; had drudged away in school hours when we would fain have been scampering down country lanes, chasing butterflies; we had found the lessons irksome, and the teachers often harsh and overbearing. But there was always playtime and freedom between school-hours. Henceforward, there would be no playtime. We had watched lad after lad leave school for work, and seen him late at night returning from work, with blackened face and hands; and as we noticed the jaded look on his face when he stood at the door and watched the children, we knew instinctively that for him playtime was ended for ever.

We stuck to our work, and grew confident

as we went on. Our class was a small one, and held only three others besides ourselves. We were placed in a position of honour round a deal table, near the master's desk. There we were seen by the whole school, and rather liked it. When we were well in front with our work, we relaxed a little, and made faces at the teachers behind their backs, to the great amusement of the school, who admired our courage and respected our importance.

We five sat in a row at one side of the table. When Freddy went away, his chair was left in its position in the middle, just as it always had been. And till we left no other lad dared to fill it.

It was hard at first. We used to turn round suddenly, half expecting, half hoping to see his quiet face bending over his work. Once, just after, we stayed at the door waiting for him to come out, and wondering why he was so long. Then we remembered.

.   .   .   .   .

The great day came at last. We were awake and up betimes that morning, busily scrubbing faces and hands, brushing clothes, and polishing boots. Then slowly we went down the road to the school. For the last time.

There was no play that morning. We stood outside in groups, talking of the coming ordeal, and wondering what the questions would be like, and how long it would last. Then, at the signal, we filed into school.

The interior had been cleaned, and the desks and forms made presentable. The maps and pictures on the walls had been carefully dusted, and the floors were guiltless of dirt. The inkpots had been - washed and refilled, and in the higher classes each lad was supplied with a new pen and a new piece of blotting paper.

Our table had been removed. In its place we found a long, new desk. We took our places, but the space in the middle was still left empty. We licked the grease off the ends of our nibs, and looked round. The lads were all in their places, silent and serious. The master, in a new suit, stood at his desk, and the teachers walked slowly up and down the room. We were waiting for the inspectors. The vicar looked in, spoke to the master and the teachers, and went out again. The master spoke to us briefly, gave the usual instructions, and asked each scholar to do his best for the honour of the school.

There came a knock at the door, and a thrill went through us. The inspectors! The minutes seemed hours as they shook hands with the schoolmaster, and as they began slowly opening their black bags we felt like convicted murderers, and yearned to rush through the doors to light and freedom.

The trial began. For several hours we answered questions, read aloud, and struggled with problems in arithmetic. We sat at a distance from each other, to prevent copying or talking, but as we furtively looked at each other we guessed that the examination was going to our satisfaction.

Time went on. Class after class was dismissed, and we heard their jubilant shouts outside. These died away, and we at our desk were left alone. At last it was over. With relieved feelings we rose and went out, with a farewell look back at the school we should enter no more.

The schoolmaster was waiting outside. He drew us aside, shook hands with each, and, in a kindlier voice than we had ever known him use, he praised us for the way we had worked during the past six months, and for our good behaviour in school. We had, he said, been a good example to the whole school. And for the first time it dawned upon us that a schoolmaster has his grievances, also.

He went on, speaking quietly; gave us good advice, hoped we should do well in after life, and enjoined us to be discontented with our present positions, and always to work on and upwards. And then he spoke of Freddy, of his blameless ways in school and out, and hoped we would always try as he did to be true and good. Then with another warm hand-shake and a cheery "good-bye, lads; now, be good!" he left us. We went home, thinking of his words, and wondering how much of his praise was due to us, or to the dear comrade who lay in Wolverhampton cemetery.

There is little more for me to say. A day or two later we learned that we had passed brilliantly, having failed in nothing. The schoolmaster gave us flattering testimonials. Armed with these we went daily to shops, factories, and warehouses, seeking work as errand boys, apprentices, or anything likely to bring in money. We soon found places, but true to a resolve made months before, we meant doing our best to find a sweeter place for us and ours than Tumblefold.

Night after night, when the day's work was over, we studied and read together indoors, or at evening classes, and became in our way good scholars. As we had resolved, so we did. By-and-bye we were separated, but the im-pulse was started, and still went on.

Jones became a carpenter, obtained a good place, and is now the energetic secretary of his trade union. He lives in quite a respectable neighbourhood; in a little cottage with a garden at the back, wherein the children playing all day long enjoy a brighter childhood than was given to their father.

Ryder, after a short spell as errand-boy, became an assistant, and is now doing well in a snug little business of his own.

Potter, the restless, tried his hand at many things: errand-boy, porter, clerk, apprentice, out-of-work, and finally landed himself on a newspaper and set to work in earnest. He is now an important man; lectures on scientific and literary subjects and is even writing a book. But he has not lost the art of grinning, as he evidenced the other day when I casually asked him if he remembered the Great Panorama.

And I; what am I?

I am but a voice and an emotion. I, too, have done well. Since those days I have learned and unlearned much. I have learned that injustice and wrong are words with meanings; that Tumblefold is not necessarily a part of the divine order of things, and that the life conditions of its denizens are not just as they ought to be.

For Tumblefold still exists, not only in Wolverhampton, but in every town and city where the greed and brutal instincts of men have trampled out of life and memory the

doings of one who said "Love one another."
Winter and summer, it is still there; the dark
labyrinth of dirty alleys and passages, with the
gutters choked up with filth and the children
playing therein.

As I look back on the dark faces of the
children of whom we four only remain as
developed human beings, they seem to me to
be imploring, entreating for light, for love,
and for life. Maybe, some day, they too shall
receive their due. It cannot, will not, always
last, if there be any faith left in men's eyes,
and any humanity in their hearts.

Always I see them; the silent, yearning
faces, lips framing questions never to be
answered, eyes seeking hopes forever invisible, and the poor throbbing brains growing
duller and heavier with undeveloped ideas and
the dead-weight of stillborn aspirations.

And, as I think of it all, I shudder thank-
fully (not selfishly; God, how can I help but
be thankful?) as I wonder how we escaped,
while they were left in the neverlifting
darkness.

Sometimes, in dreams, I live through it all
again, and I wake with an agonising dread
which holds me from looking through my
window lest I should meet the same dark,
hideous stretch, and, seeing the damned faces

at the doors, know myself to be once more with them and of them.

Then I remember, and am glad. I know that our gain was not their loss.

And their day may yet come.

THE END

Lightning Source UK Ltd.
Milton Keynes UK
UKOW06f1905080416

271888UK00014B/290/P